Joys and Sorrows at
NATHANIEL CHRISTIAN ORPHANAGE
in Romania

*Mariana &
Mihaela Gheorgheş,
and Ioana Diculov*

HeartBridge

JOHNNY MILLER

ISBN: 978-1-885270-73-3

Cover Design: Gloria Miller

First Printing: March 2008

Printed in the USA

For more information about Christian Aid Ministries, see page 268.

To order additional copies of *HeartBridge* please contact:

TGS International
PO Box 355
Berlin, Ohio 44610 USA
Phone: 330·893·4828
Fax: 330·893·2305

HeartBridge

JOHNNY MILLER

ACKNOWLEDGMENT

This story of our first year in Romania is written with grateful acknowledgment to God, who called us to so great a work, and to my loving wife and partner Ruth, who became Mama to these children in a very true sense of the word. Nor can I forget the vital roles played by our son Franklin and daughters Ida Jane and Caroline. Their work was invaluable in winning hearts. A special acknowledgement also goes to our Romanian staff, who took us in, overlooked our blunders, and loved us into feeling at home among them.

DEDICATION

I dedicate this book to the children of the Nathaniel Christian Orphanage. These God mightily used to teach me and to refine my life. To them I shall ever be indebted.

Johnny Miller

NATHANIEL CHRISTIAN

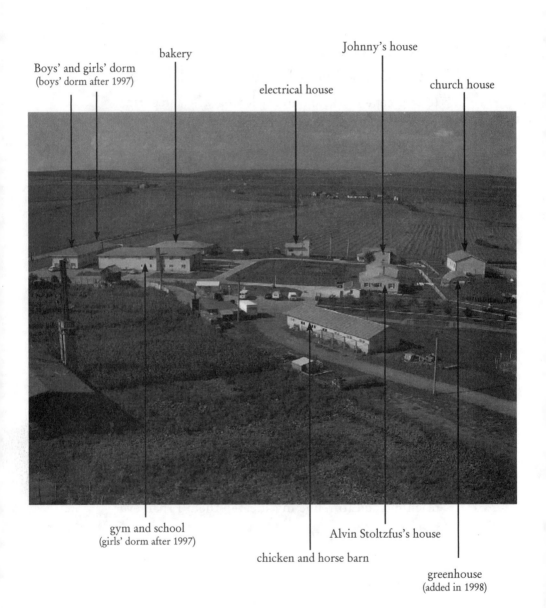

Boys' and girls' dorm
(boys' dorm after 1997)

bakery

electrical house

Johnny's house

church house

gym and school
(girls' dorm after 1997)

chicken and horse barn

Alvin Stoltzfus's house

greenhouse
(added in 1998)

ORPHANAGE COMPOUND

wood shop and
machinery storage

school house
(built in 1998)

dairy barn

feed mill

milk processing plant

TABLE OF
CONTENTS

PROLOGUE

The massive three-story building loomed bleak and uninviting against the horizon, a stark monument to communism. Its formidable iron gate blocked the view into the courtyard. No foreigner had ever set foot within these cold concrete walls that reportedly housed more than four hundred unwanted children. Now four American men wanted to see what life was like within.

A guard answered their knock and allowed them to step inside his guardhouse while he called his superior. It was early February, 1990, and winter held Romania in its frigid grip. The men pulled their overcoats tighter, glad for the limited shelter of the guardhouse. Just two months before, they would never have been permitted to come this far. But communist dictator Nicolae Ceauşescu had been overthrown and executed by firing squad six weeks earlier, culminating Romania's struggle to throw off the yoke of communism which had oppressed her people for forty-five years, and the old rules were changing.

The guard ushered David Troyer, Paul Weaver, Amos Martin, and Paul Miller to the main entrance of the orphanage, where the supervisor led them through cement hallways echoing with children's cries. Dim light filtered in through sparse windows, assisted here and there by the glare of a bare bulb dangling from the high concrete ceiling.

The supervisor led them through the dormitories, where children crowded together on rusted metal beds. There was no other furniture, and barely enough room to walk. The men tried to mask their shock when they realized many of the children were half naked. Quite a few were also barefoot, and the room temperature was in the low fifties. The corners were soiled with human waste, which, combined with the unmistakable odor of soaked bedding, produced an overpowering stench that even the penetrating cold could not abate.

A child began to cry piteously, then stopped suddenly when he was roughly smacked by a worker and commanded to shut up. In the next room a group of children was seated about a low table with metal graniteware mugs in their hands. Bedlam erupted as a worker entered carrying a bucket of watery soup. Mugs clanked as children jumped up and stretched toward the bucket. The larger children shoved the smaller ones rudely aside, screaming to be first. Many frantically slurped from their mugs and stretched them forth again, crying for more.

The American visitors fought tears. These children responded like abused, neglected animals.

In yet another room they saw four small children tied to a single bed. Some had soiled themselves and were in dire need of attention. They didn't even turn their heads as the visitors walked past.

Finally the visitors were shown into the basement. As they entered the room, frightened children screamed and lunged as far from the workers as their restraints would allow. The fetid smell was unbearable, and the children's cries rent the visitors' hearts. The men were weeping now. Several children were obviously ill and were reduced to skin and bones. Many seemed near death.

The men had seen enough. The heavy silence that filled their van as they left the orphanage and its suffering children behind was broken only by an occasional blowing of a nose or clearing of a throat. Though tears blurred their vision, nothing could blur the pictures in their minds. Their hearts were filled with indignation as they recalled the spectacular palace Ceauşescu had built for himself in Bucureşti, while 240,000 precious Romanian children languished in orphanages like the one they had just left.

Something had to be done. Who would hear the cry of these orphans? Who would plead their cause?

CHAPTER 1

THE WALK

Bill stood in the open doorway of the moving train with his wife Ellen behind him. Tears streamed down their faces as the train rolled past the crowd. They waved their arms in a farewell salute to the orphanage children they loved so dearly, the loyal staff, and the Romanian friends who had come to bid them farewell. After two years of directing the Nathaniel Christian Orphanage in Suceava,* Romania, the Mullets were returning to their home in America.

My wife and I followed the departing train, waving. Tears blurred our vision as we stumbled along through the snow. We stopped. It was futile to continue. Sobbing, Ruth turned to me and said, "This isn't right! We should be the ones leaving, not them!"

This walk had actually begun months earlier at our home in Ohio. I had stopped in for a few minutes between plumbing jobs, and my wife Ruth told me she had received a call from a secretary at Christian Aid Ministries (CAM).

"What did she want?" I asked, assuming it had something to do with their ministerial committee, of which I was a member.

---

* Please see glossary on pages 263-265 for pronunciations of Romanian words.

Ruth filled another jar with the spicy salsa she was canning before replying. "Paul and Orpha Weaver would like to take us out for supper Tuesday evening. We're supposed to meet them at six o'clock at the North Canton Holiday Inn. The secretary said to call and let them know if we can make it."

"Good," I replied as I headed toward the door and an appointment with a customer. "Call and tell them we'll be there."

"They specifically asked for you," Ruth replied sweetly. "I think you should call."

"Please," I said, "you call. I'm in a hurry." I headed on out the door, climbed into the work van, and hurried off.

Tuesday evening arrived, and I rushed home from work. Glancing at the kitchen clock, I realized there would barely be time to shower, change, and get to the meeting place by six, but I hurried, and soon we were headed for North Canton.

"Why do you suppose they invited us?" Ruth asked.

"Their wedding anniversary was last week," I replied offhandedly. "That's all I can think of." After a pause I added, "The motel is a big place. How are we supposed to find them?"

"I'm sure I don't know," Ruth replied. "What did they say when you called them?"

My head jerked around in surprise, and I gave my wife a startled look. "Why, I never called. I thought you did. Didn't you?"

"Well, no," Ruth answered innocently. "I just figured you were going to call since they asked for you."

"I can't believe this!" I sputtered. "I have no idea where to meet them! How embarrassing!"

With many misgivings, we arrived at the Holiday Inn. I glanced at my watch. Eight minutes past six. I chose one of the huge parking lot's many entrances and crept through the rows of parked cars, looking carefully to the left, then to the right. *How will we ever find Paul and Orpha in this mess when we don't even know what kind of car they drive?* I thought. *Perhaps they aren't even here since I never called back to confirm our plans. How could I have been so negligent?*

"Oh, there they are!" blurted Ruth.

"Where?" I asked, looking about in disbelief.

"Right there in front of you. Be careful or you'll bump into them," she chuckled.

Paul and Orpha were waiting in their van right beside the main entrance. Paul, grinning broadly, rolled down his window and asked, "Would you like to park your car and ride with us?"

"Sure," I replied, relieved that things had worked out in spite of my blunder. Paul and Orpha had a good laugh when we told them what had happened.

"I know how much you enjoy Chinese food," Paul turned to me, "so I thought we'd take you to a special restaurant I found. I hope you'll like it."

"I'm sure I will," I said.

In a short time we found ourselves chatting comfortably over a variety of delicious foods. Our discussion ranged from home and children to church and work. There was a lull in the conversation as we finished our meal. Paul looked first to me and then to my wife. "Have you been wondering why we asked you to join us this evening?"

I leaned forward, eyebrows arched in an unspoken question. Paul hurried on.

"I won't keep you waiting long," he began, looking across the table. "Ruth, are you aware that CAM has an orphanage in Romania where fifty-three precious souls live? These little children need the direction of a man to become like a father to them, to love them, to guide them, and to teach them biblical truths to prepare them for life. We feel your husband has the qualifications needed to fill this place in their lives. What would you say if we were to ask him—in fact, we are asking him—to seriously consider moving to Romania to be the director of the Nathaniel Christian Orphanage?"

My head bowed lower and lower as I listened. My mind raced. *This is ridiculous! There's no way! What would happen to the plumbing business I've struggled twenty years to build? And I'm a deacon in our church! There's no way I can shirk that responsibility! Then there's the mortgage on our place. How will it ever get paid if we move to Romania?*

Paul had ceased speaking, and there was dead silence around the table. Paul asked, "Did that shock you?"

I sat with my head still bowed, too stunned for words.

"No," said Ruth, "this didn't shock me. I knew it this afternoon."

I gave a start and stared at my dear wife.

"God told me," she stated matter-of-factly. "I was washing dishes when suddenly I sensed in my spirit that we were going to be asked to move to Romania."

"But you never told me!" I sputtered, dazed.

"I know," said Ruth. "I'm sorry. I guess there just didn't seem to be a right moment."

The next two hours were filled with rapid-fire discussion. Paul spelled out what CAM expected from the director of the orphanage and outlined the need for a co-pastor in the newly formed Nathaniel Christian Church. He spoke of the children, their needs, and their future. The list seemed endless. While we asked question after question, the Holy Spirit spoke to our hearts and opened our minds to the possibility that God was calling us to this work.

We drove home sobered, having promised to pray about the matter and to seriously consider their request.

The next several days were soul-searching ones as we laid open our lives before the Lord. We wanted to follow Him above all else, and yet . . . we had to be sure. Soon, however, we began to feel a sense of direction in our spirits. As we discussed the orphanage and the move to Romania, we caught ourselves saying *when* instead of *if.*

First we spoke of this call with our married son Dwight, then with our eighteen-year-old daughter Ida Jane. She had been personally praying about entering into some type of work where she would be ministering to others. Was this an answer to her prayers?

"If we move to Romania, do you think I am old enough to help work with the children?" she asked.

Next we approached our twenty-four-year-old, unmarried son, John, who no longer lived at home. He wasn't so sure he liked the idea of Mom and Dad, Ida, Franklin, and Caroline moving so far away.

Our oldest daughter, Vicki, married to Nathan Yoder, was living in Costa Rica. We placed a call to share with them the possibility of our moving to Romania. They encouraged us and promised to pray that we would find God's will in the matter.

We felt it was now time to approach our youngest children—nine-year-old Caroline and twelve-year-old Franklin. Caroline thought it might be a neat experience. But when Franklin realized we were seriously thinking of moving to far-off Romania, he burst into tears. Through his sobs he told Caroline, "We'll just come back in a couple of years and be weird little missionary kids!"

"Now, don't take it so hard," I said, trying to comfort him. "We still have to pray and seek God's will. And we haven't even asked Brother Leonard about it. I really don't know what he will say."

Franklin was now crying in earnest. "Oh, you know how it will be. God and Leonard—they'll both just say 'yes,' " he sobbed pathetically.

Several days passed. Ruth, as was her habit, stopped at Franklin's bedside to tell him goodnight. As she came near his bed, Franklin spoke. "It's all right, Mom. About Romania, I mean. In my devotions I found a verse in Job 13:15 that says, 'Though he slay me, yet will I trust in Him . . .' "

Ruth had to smile in spite of Franklin's seriousness, but she realized it was the part about trusting that had caught his attention, and not necessarily the part about being slain.

After a week we shared our call with our bishop, Leonard Overholt, and with the church. Pros and cons were thoroughly discussed, and the church was asked to vote on whether to allow their deacon to move to Romania. A co-minister asked what percentage of the total church vote I would consider to be clearance for us to leave. "Should it be fifty-one percent, seventy-five percent, or eighty percent?" he asked. "You understand," he continued, "that it's not likely a church the size of ours will give you a unanimous vote."

I responded that the ministry should make that determination, not me. Since God had placed this call within our hearts, I was confident that He would see us through these details.

The vote was taken, and for the first time in many years I did not assist in counting the ballots, since the vote involved my family. Brother Leonard approached me after the votes were tallied.

"Do you still feel the call to move to Romania?" he asked.

"Yes, we do," I answered, knowing I spoke for my whole family.

Brother Leonard nodded soberly. "Well," he said, "the vote was unanimous."

We had been granted a two-year leave of absence from our church responsibilities. This affirmation lent warmth and blessing to our plans.

Several weeks after we gave CAM our answer, Silvia Tărniceriu came to pay us a visit. She had grown up in Iaşi, Romania, and had been active in Bible smuggling and teaching youth while the country was still under communism. She now poured her energetic spirit into working for CAM. Silvia brought pictures of the orphanage children and told us about them. Her stories helped Franklin, Caroline, and Ida Jane visualize living and working among these children. Caroline found herself gazing at several photos and dreaming about becoming friends with these girls.

The evening came to an end far too soon for our family. Just as Silvia was about to leave, she grew very serious. "You know," she said, looking at the attentive faces of our family gathered about her, "these orphanage children need someone to live with them and love them for ten years." Then, looking straight at me, she added, "You'll stay in Romania for ten years, yes?"

Ten years was unthinkable, but I didn't say so.

A month later CAM sent Ruth and me to Romania for a week of orientation. We met the orphanage director, Bill Mullet, his wife Ellen, and the orphanage children. Bill explained how the orphanage operated and showed me around the city of Suceava. Meanwhile, Ellen familiarized Ruth with the little gray house where we would be living, right on the orphanage compound. We would be close to the children at all times. We were introduced to tall, strong Ionică Bădiliță, a Pentecostal pastor and the Romanian director of the orphanage. Ionică also represented the orphanage before the Romanian government and kept abreast of all the necessary legal work.

We returned to our family in Ohio with a much greater understanding of the huge responsibility before us. Were we really equipped for so great a task?

We had much to accomplish in the two months before our moving date. Our oldest son, Dwight, would assume operation of the family plumbing business with assistance from our younger son, John. We had to make financial arrangements, as well as myriads of other decisions. What should we take, and what must be left behind? We crated up personal items for shipment to

Romania. We visited family and church members one last time and said our farewells.

Finally January 14, 1997, arrived. Friends and family gathered at the Cleveland Hopkins Airport to see us off. As the call to board the waiting plane echoed over the intercom, a brother led those assembled in singing, "God Be With You Till We Meet Again," and tears began to flow. It was so difficult to leave! But at the urging of the airline attendant, we pulled ourselves away from our loved ones and boarded the plane.

Welcomed by the Nathaniel Orphanage children

Exhaustion took over and we slept during the night as we crossed the Atlantic. Flying east through seven time zones made for a short night, but a very long day.

In Bucureşti we were met by a CAM employee whose job was to get us across that sprawling city in time to catch the train for Suceava. The seven-hour train ride north was filled with anxious anticipation as we approached our new home, a new language, and a new life. Finally we arrived at the Suceava station, where a group of well-wishers welcomed us warmly. Silvia was among them.

During the next two weeks we stuck very close to Bill and Ellen. We wanted to learn from them all we possibly could. There was so much we just did not know. Who was to oversee the meal-times? Who was to lead in prayer, and in what language? Where was the director supposed to sit during dinner? How, and at what time, do you put a family of fifty-three children to

Bill, Ellen, and daughter departing by train

bed for the night? Who gets them up in the morning? When do they have devotions? How do you get them ready for church? Who disciplines them when they are naughty? Who orders the groceries for so large a family? Do they eat the same foods we do? The list of things to learn seemed endless, and what was worse, we had to learn them through an interpreter.

All too soon the day of Bill and Ellen's departure came. We bade them farewell, and the Suceava-Bucureşti train rolled out, leaving us standing beside the tracks, staring south through our tears—alone, yet not alone, for He who had called us had also promised never to leave us nor forsake us.

CHAPTER 2

BEGINNINGS

Ruth and I soon realized that the Nathaniel Christian Orphanage was, in reality, an institution. However, we felt a deep desire to make this institution as warm and homey as possible. The callous chill of the state-operated orphanages in Romania was a continuing blight we had no wish to duplicate. Surely God had something better in store for these dear children, and by His grace we would implement it.

I soon found out I was expected to continue the routines set in motion by the former directors. I was amazed to see just how important these routines were to the children. It gave them a sense of security and helped them accept me as their new director. It also gave them a sense of belonging—something most important in the lives of abandoned children and orphans.

Before each meal the children lined up in the hallway leading into the dining room. Twenty-seven girls formed the head of this long, lively line, and twenty-six boys followed. They stood expectantly, waiting for the director to ring his hand bell signaling them to proceed to their assigned seats, then filed to their places with the girls on the left sides of the tables and the boys opposite. Daycare workers usually sat at the head and foot of each table.

Once in their places, they remained standing for prayer, which was led by the director or by someone designated by him. Romanian culture demands respect for religion, so one either stands or kneels for prayer, but never sits. To remain seated during prayer is considered quite irreverent indeed!

First director David Yoder lines up the children for the dining room.

The director's assigned seat was reserved for me at the head of the first table. This became the "throne" from which I "reigned" over the dining room, and the bell became my scepter of authority.

Ruth occupied the chair reserved for the "queen" at the other end of this table. Sharing two meals with the children became a daily routine that they enjoyed as much as we did. This was a time to connect with the children—to learn their names and to recognize their individual character traits.

I had difficulty getting used to the sheer volume of noise produced by fifty-three energetic children as they ate and talked together. Again and again I tried to get them to speak more softly and not all at once, but to no avail. Ruth came to their rescue one day.

"Just listen!" she exclaimed. "These are happy sounds."

It was true. Their chatter reminded me of one big happy family gathered around the tables. The animated discussions were about events important to their young lives.

I listened carefully and heard Beti from the next table tell how she had gotten the best of Costică, who had been teasing her. From the third table, Costică aptly defended his position in spite of the good-natured ribbing he received from Ionela. Marinel told of his plans to visit folks who had befriended him while he was a homeless street boy in Suceava. Our Romanian director, Ionică, explained that when he found the right horse for the children, we were going to buy it. Marius gave a vivid description of just how much fun it would be to gallop all over the farm once that horse became ours.

In spite of my discomfort at the noise, I had to agree with my wife that these were indeed happy sounds. As the meal came to an end, plates and drinking glasses were neatly stacked near the head of each table and the utensils were placed in a bowl. All the children were responsible for helping clear the tables. A new team of children was selected each day to help the cooks wash and dry the dishes, while others wiped the tables. Another group was assigned to sweep the dining room floor.

I rang the bell, paused, and waited for the children to quiet down. I then asked the child whose name was written on the calendar to choose a song. Meals always ended with a song of praise offered to God. Then, armed with my legendary bell, I walked through the dining room "dinging" a dismissal for each table in turn, thus maintaining a semblance of order in spite of the children's urgency to rush from the dining room to more interesting pursuits.

Another valuable tradition that enriched the lives of our children was a daily devotional period following breakfast. The morning daycare worker for the boys, either Nenea Geo or Nenea Daniel, read a portion of Scripture and followed it up with an explanation or a personal experience that emphasized the Bible principle. A closing prayer and song concluded our morning devotions.

Respect for those older than one's self is a valued part of Romanian culture. Men who worked for the orphanage were referred to as *nenea*, meaning "uncle." Women were called *tanti*, meaning "aunt." Children who referred to a worker by a first name without this respectful prefix immediately earned a serious reprimand from the nearest daycare worker.

Devotions were also held each evening before the children were tucked into their beds. Often this included a bedtime story, which the children dearly loved. They never tired of stories and often begged to be read to.

By choice, my office was located along the hallway where the traffic was heaviest. I kept the door open unless engaged in some private interview. This proved to be an invaluable asset, as it was an open invitation for the children to drop in for a visit whenever they felt the need. They frequently stopped in when they had a problem or to share a grievance or disagreement. At other times it was a pair of glasses that needed a screw from my repair kit. Sometimes it was a minor injury that needed attention. Many an ailment was healed with a Band-Aid, a healing touch, or a word of encouragement. I fell in love with these darling children, and ministering to their hurts became my passion.

Down at the little gray house which was our home, Ruth quickly discovered the joy of having orphanage children drop in throughout the day, often accompanied by a daycare worker. Imagine six eager little girls all talking at once as they tried to bridge the language barrier between their beloved Romanian tanti and Sora (Sister) Ruth, whom they were just beginning to know. The children spoke only what English they'd learned in their English classes, which started in second grade, though they were rapidly improving with so many Americans to practice on.

Ida Jane and Caroline were intriguing to the children as well.

Ida found she could help out in the orphanage by doing laundry and working in the kitchen. This allowed her to practice her Romanian, as did her daily language classes with Silvia. Caroline, who was only several months older than the oldest of the orphanage girls, also quickly picked up some Romanian.

In the meantime, Franklin was down at the farm blending with the boys, who quickly became his friends. Language wasn't much more than a slight hindrance for him, and he was soon helping with the chores and playing with the boys. The twins, Ionuţ and Nicu, were full of action and very outgoing, while Pavel and Marius were more reserved and shy. At times their fun took a serious turn.

As boys are wont to do, they got into a rather innocent fight. Marius tossed an ear of corn at Ionuţ, and within minutes there was a major corn battle in progress. More boys joined in, quickly forming two opposing teams. Franklin was just as determined as the other boys to defend his fellow corn-throwers against the opposing team. All went well until the farm director, Alvin Stoltzfus, noticed the mess they were making.

"Okay, boys," he said kindly, no doubt recalling his own boyhood days, "stop throwing and begin cleaning up." Alvin turned and went back to his work. Franklin still held a good throwing ear in his hand and couldn't resist the temptation for one last fling. The ear flipped slowly end over end as it sailed in a graceful arch straight toward Pavel, who looked up a split second before it arrived. The butt of that full ear of corn caught him straight in the eye. In a second Pavel was writhing on the ground in agony. He tried hard to keep from crying before his peers, but he couldn't. The pain was just too severe.

Franklin rushed over to him, apologizing all the while, but Pavel kept screaming over and over again, "I can't see, I can't see!"

Fear gripped Franklin's heart. He moved his hand in front of Pavel's injured eye, and in desperation asked, "Can you see my hand?"

"No," replied Pavel between sobs. "I can't see anything out of my eye." Franklin hurriedly guided him up to the orphanage for medical help while a group of very sober boys began picking up the loose ears of corn they had helped scatter about.

Franklin felt so terrible that he, too, had to cry. He insisted on going along with Pavel to the hospital. There, the examining doctor determined that in spite of the eyeball and retina being severely bruised, there was a good chance for complete recovery if Pavel would take it easy and wear a patch for several days to rest his injured eye.

This incident became a vital object lesson for Franklin and the boys on the importance of immediate obedience. But the near disaster turned into a blessing as it brought Pavel out of his shy reserve, and he and Franklin soon became best friends.

In putting action to our prayers about making the Nathaniel Orphanage a real home for these children, Ruth and I began going up to the orphanage to help get the children settled into their beds for the night. Together we went from room to room and talked with each child for several minutes. We enjoyed tucking their covers up under their chins and telling them goodnight.

After several evenings of spending two to three minutes with each of the fifty-three children, Ruth and I realized we were neglecting our own children. We could ill afford to spend several hours each evening telling these precious children goodnight, so Ruth and I decided to divide the duties. Ruth would go to the girls' dorm, and I to the boys'. This would cut our time in half and allow us more freedom to connect with our own children.

The first night we tried this, though, I had only made it into the second room when Marian, with a hurt look on his face, asked, "Where is Sora Ruth? Isn't she coming tonight?"

"Yes," chimed in Iosif, "I want to tell her goodnight too."

Over in the girls' dorm Ruth was encountering the same problem. "Sora Ruth, where is Nenea Johnny? Isn't he coming to tell us goodnight?" asked the girls.

These children had been abandoned by their mothers. Many had never even met, much less known, a loving father. They were starved for love and attention. So the following evening we again made our rounds together to tell the children goodnight, and they were happy once more.

Some children really didn't know how to respond to our love. How do you hug a child who doesn't know how? Some children clung to us quite literally, while others clung to us verbally as they invented questions to hold our attention as long as possible. But we were always conscious of others waiting in the remaining rooms, and of Caroline, Franklin, and Ida Jane waiting for their mom and dad down at the little gray house.

A very troubled Mariana at bedtime

One evening we bade the last child goodnight and were on the way home when I heard Ruth sigh as she said, "I feel just like the little old lady who lived in a shoe and had so many children that she didn't know what to do."

Our bedtime ministry continued to grow in importance as time passed, but with it came unanswerable questions. How do you comfort a little girl you find quietly sobbing into her pillow when you can barely speak her language? Was she remembering her mother who died when she was only four, or her father who became a bitter alcoholic as he tried to drown his sorrows? Was she recalling scenes from her past too painful to bear? Were we pulling emotional scabs off old wounds and causing more hurt than healing? We hoped that, if we continued ministering, we could eventually bring healing to their bruised hearts.

Because of their tragic past experiences, these children entertained fears not normal for young children. Once, while Ruth was telling seven-year-old Andi goodnight, she stood close to his bunk and reached up to rumple his hair affectionately. As she stretched to kiss him goodnight, he placed his arms about her neck in a tight embrace and asked the question that was burning in his lonely little heart. "Mama Ruth," he whispered, "you go America?"

After arriving in Romania, we had talked about our original plan to stay two years. Already we knew that would not be enough, so we'd decided to leave the length of our stay open-ended. When Ruth answered Andi, "No, I stay Romania," his cup of joy overflowed! With his arms still clutching Ruth in a tight embrace, he catapulted from his top bunk, nearly bowling Ruth over backward. All he had ever known were painful separations. The fear of abandonment was very real for Andi and for many others like him. As this realization dawned upon us, we determined in our hearts to do everything we could to allay their fears. We would try to share with these children our home life, our personal activities, and our hearts whenever possible. We wanted them to feel like part of our family.

One evening, somewhat later than usual, I was tiptoeing from room to room. Most of the boys were already asleep. I skipped them, but here and there I found one still awake and spent several moments telling him goodnight. Quietly I entered yet another room—and was startled by what I saw. Little nine-year-old Marian Biţica lay on his back with his eyes tightly shut. He was gripping the back of his head with his left hand and covering his forehead with his right forearm. He rolled his head, neck, and upper body back and forth rapidly, as though trying desperately to rock himself to sleep.

I watched him in silence for several moments. The motion appeared so unnatural—it no doubt stemmed from some inner turmoil from his tragic past. I bent silently above him and gently touched his arm. The rocking motion ceased immediately, and his eyes flew open in surprise. Then a big smile spread over his face. He called my name in a soft tone that told me he had waited and hoped that I would come, but had finally given up. Marian began asking a barrage of questions far faster than I could possibly answer them. I wondered if he was really searching for answers to his questions, or just coercing me to spend a few more coveted moments with him. When my answers finally caught up with his questions, I bent over to kiss him goodnight. His thin little arms went around my neck and he pulled my face down against his. He whispered into my ear, "Tata (Daddy) Johnny, I love you. God bless you. You are my friend."

On another evening, as I approached the rooms near the far end of the girl's dorm, ten-year-old Elena Biţica called out, "Tata Johnny, come here." As I stood on my tiptoes to bring my face level with her bunk, she reached out a thin arm, encircled my neck, and drew me close. She whispered into my ear. "Tata Johnny, I want you to . . ." But my poor Romanian was too limited to understand what she wanted. Again and again, with deep feeling, she repeated the same phrase, but I still could not understand what she needed. After several attempts, Elena was ready to give up when help came from an unexpected source. Cute, round-faced Maria climbed out of her bed on the far side of the hallway and came shyly to offer her aid. Her eyes bright with understanding, Maria said in her best English, "Nenea Johnny, Elena is ask you pray her."

"Oh!" I replied. "Thank you for your help." Maria smiled

sweetly, most pleased at being able to help Nenea Johnny, then scampered back into her bed.

I turned once again to Elena and said, "Now I understand. You are asking me to pray for you. Is that right?"

"Yes," responded Elena, "will you?"

"What would you like for me to pray?" I asked.

"That I not dream," was her burdened response.

Then it hit me. This was the oldest of the four Biţica children. She had seen with her own eyes the brutal beating and murder of her mother by her father. She, along with her smaller brother and sisters, had cried out in defense of their mother, but their father would not listen. Finally he had threatened to kill them all if they didn't cease their pleadings. On that fateful night in their little house in nearby Mitoc, this tender girl had heard the screams and seen the blood of her dying mother. The police had come and taken her father to prison, and she hadn't seen him since.

Now she was afraid to sleep and was asking me to pray that she would no longer be tormented with horrible dreams. Standing near her bedside, her arm around my neck, I prayed to the One who mends broken hearts. "O God, please touch Elena with your love. Help her to trust you, to know you. Help her to forget her horrible past. Protect her from bad dreams and fill her with thoughts of your marvelous grace."

And the just God of heaven heard the heartcry of this little girl.

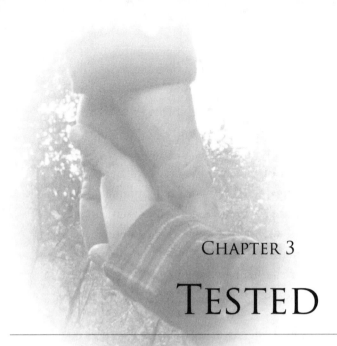

CHAPTER 3

TESTED

There is a honeymoon period in new beginnings, but a time of testing always follows, and ours was just around the corner.

It was suppertime, and the children were seated in their usual places. The meal and discussions were in full swing. Ruth caught my eye from her end of the table, motioning for me to look at one of the smaller girls. Four-year-old Ioana sat with her elbows on the table, her face cupped in her hands, and a look in her eyes which plainly said, "Leave me alone!"

Upon inquiry, I learned that this little slip a girl was upset because she had been denied the exclusive privilege of sitting beside our daughter, Caroline. She sat thus in resolute obstinance, refusing to take even one small bite of her food. She, along with the other children, knew the rules quite well: Take a little of everything that is served, and eat what you put on your plate.

Ruth tried to coax her into eating her food, but Ioana pouted even more and averted her gaze disrespectfully. With a nod, Ruth turned the situation over to me.

I left my chair to talk to Ioana, but all my explanations and entreaties had no more effect than Ruth's. As soon as I went back to my place, she was pouting again. I returned and began lifting

Ioana from the bench. That did it! She turned into a little tigress, grabbing everything possible to keep me from taking her out of her seat. At the same time, she let everyone in the dining room know that, in spite of her lack of recent nourishment, there was no strength lacking in her lungs. She howled! I felt my neck and ears turn several shades of pink as I realized all eyes were upon me. I imagined they were all wondering why this new director was tormenting an innocent little child. I sat her back on the bench firmly. I informed her that if she wanted to remain where she was, she'd better straighten up, quit the pouting, and eat her food.

Ioana continued to cry and cast nasty looks in my direction with her big, wet, brown eyes. I let her pout for several more minutes while I contemplated what I should do next. I could almost read the minds of the workers and children. *If Ioana can so easily overcome this new director, we will be in for a jolly good time indeed!*

My mind was made up, and I rose slowly and deliberately. I strode purposefully to where Ioana sat, reached down, and gently disengaged her clutching fingers from the table's edge. Next I extracted her feet from where she had curled them beneath the bench. I took her shrieking, writhing form into my arms and returned to my seat at the head of the table. The rest of the children had paused to observe, but now returned to their meal. Ioana continued scowling at everyone as I asked for her plate to be passed to me. I tried to help her eat, but Ioana's jaws were locked tight.

Our interpreter, Lucian, walked past just then, and I asked if he would please help me. He stooped down until he was eye level with Ioana. He pleaded with her in his most persuasive Romanian. "Nenea Johnny said that if you don't stop pouting and eat your food, you will receive a spanking for your stubbornness. The decision is yours. You don't have to eat your food, but then you will receive a punishment," he explained soberly.

Several of the children, not wanting Ioana to be punished, also tried to persuade her to eat. "Just a wee little bit," they coaxed. But Ioana refused and stuck her little pug nose defiantly into the air.

A worker had provided a treat of peppermint candy for each of the children. As the dish came close, Ioana grabbed a

Sweet little Ioana

piece. "No," I explained. "If you do not eat your food, you may not have candy." I took it from her.

Supper was soon finished, and the children were dismissed following their usual song. I started down the hall toward my office with a defiant Ioana in tow. I asked my wife to accompany me. Before we reached the office, we were intercepted by one of our daycare workers. She knelt down beside Ioana and made cooing, motherly, Romanian noises. Then, wrapping her arms about Ioana, she stood and turned as if to carry her away. I immediately realized what was about to happen and thought I'd best nip this type of interference in the bud. So politely, yet firmly, I asked to have Ioana back and continued to my office, where I held her on my lap and spoke with her.

Together Ruth and I explained that because of her stubbornness she must receive a punishment. With that, I bent her over my knee and gave her a spanking, carefully matching the intensity with the smallness of her size. I continued talking to her, explaining once more the need for obedience. After drying her tears, I presented her with the peppermint. Ioana slowly opened the candy wrapper. Thoughtfully, as though trying to figure it all out, she placed the candy into her mouth. Then for the first time she looked up at me. As we sat there gazing into each other's eyes, something happened in our hearts—we became friends!

Following this incident, Ioana delighted in sitting near her "Nenea Johnny" at mealtimes. She would clean up every scrap from her plate, then, in her own darling way, place her tiny hands upon the top of her head and exclaim how tall she had grown because she had eaten all her food. She would jabber away with all the expression her lilting voice and shining brown eyes could muster. As soon as her plate was clean, she would ask if she could sit on my lap, where she reigned supremely as my "bell girl." She could hardly wait until I gave her permission to ring the bell, signaling the time for our closing song. Following dismissal, she would march triumphantly to the kitchen and reverently place the bell in its corner of the cupboard.

A week later I was tested in yet another way, again at the supper table. I asked Nenea Geo to lead in prayer, but just before shutting my eyes, I saw to my horror that all our glasses contained thick, clabbered buttermilk! I prayed my own private prayer. "Lord, you know all about my squeamish stomach, and you know there is no way I'll ever get this stuff down and make it stay down. You also know, Lord, that I'm supposed to be an example to these children. How can I force these children to drink this terrible stuff when I absolutely can't?"

After Nenea Geo said, "Amen," I sat down slowly so as to put off the ordeal as long as possible. I needn't have worried. Every child scooped up his glass and chugged it down with glee! They knew what it was and loved it. I took a feigned sip and suppressed a shudder, hoping none of the children had noticed.

Davucu, sitting next to me, placed his empty glass back on the table and smacked his lips. He looked up at me with the sweetest smile and asked, "Nenea Johnny, may I drink your buttermilk too?"

I wanted to hug him then and there, but instead I said, "Well, if you're sure to clean up your plate, I guess I'll let you have it."

The buttermilk test

So Davucu got a second glass of thick homemade buttermilk, and I got out of a sticky situation. We were both pleased with the transaction.

Several days later Ionică, our Romanian director, entered my office, bringing a belt and nine-year-old Iliuță with him. He motioned for Iliuță to have a seat, then turned and shut the office door. I wondered just what was wrong now.

It turned out that Iliuță had accidentally been hit in the head by a basketball while playing in the gym. The other boys had teased him for crying, and he had lost his temper, cursing the boys with foul language. Ionică had been informed and was ready to deal with the situation. He explained to me that this young man had a history of losing his temper and needed our help.

Iliuță's personal appearance was always neat. He seemed pleasant and very much in command. In general, he was not a discipline problem. "But," said Ionică, "when he becomes angry, he loses all control. Such mistakes must be corrected," he continued, "or it will hinder his development."

Turning to Iliuţă, he asked, "How many stripes do you think would be appropriate for what you have done?"

Sniffling and eyeing the belt, Iliuţă said wistfully, "Oh, I suppose two."

"What?" asked Ionică, his voice rising. "For those horrible curses you used?" Quickly Iliuţă changed the proposed count to four. Ionică agreed, provided Iliuţă returned to each of the boys he had cursed and asked forgiveness.

Ionică proceeded to mete out the punishment, but only after promising that for each additional recurrence there would be one additional stripe until he learned to control his temper.

Following the punishment, the three of us knelt together and prayed for cleansing and forgiveness and that God would help Iliuţă overcome his anger. As we got up from our knees, I couldn't help but give Iliuţă a hug. I commended him for admitting his wrong and for taking his punishment like a man. I also told him, "I'll be praying that Jesus will remind you of this incident the next time Satan tempts you to become angry."

That night as we were tucking the children into bed, I gave Iliuţă an extra squeeze. Ruth whispered into his ear as she bent to kiss him goodnight, "I heard you had trouble today, and I'm sorry, but I hope it will not happen again."

Iliuţă, who knew not whether his own mother was dead or alive, gave her a heart-warming response. He smiled at Ruth and said seriously, "I did wrong, and now it's paid for. I'll try to do better."

The next time Ionică brought a child into my office, it was Adi. His godly mother had succumbed to cancer while he was still too young to remember. Now six years old, he was still so short that his big, sober eyes barely reached above the rim of my desk as he awaited his fate. He was usually a shy, well-behaved boy, and I wondered what he could possibly have done wrong. Then Ionică began to explain the problem.

"Adi came into my office asking if it would be possible for him to become the director of this orphanage. I asked him which office he wanted, mine or Nenea Johnny's, and he said he wanted yours." I glanced from Adi to Ionică in amazement and with relief noted the twinkle in Ionică's eyes. A faint hint of a smile played around the corners of his mouth. He bit his lip to keep a straight face as he continued, "Now, what are you going to say to his request?"

I leaned forward and met Adi's deep, sober gaze. "Before you can become the director of this orphanage," I explained as I placed my hand on my head, "you must grow to be at least this big." Struggling to maintain a serious countenance, I added, "You must also have white hair, as I do." I looked again at Ionică. Our eyes met and we smiled over the top of Adi's bowed head while he contemplated his lack of qualifications for the position. Little Adi thought it over for a moment. Now that he better understood the requirements, he thought it best to leave the directorship of the Nathaniel Orphanage to others. Excusing himself, he proceeded to his dorm, where his daycare worker was waiting to put him to bed for his afternoon nap.

Another day, Ionică showed up at my office with two ten-year-old girls in tow. Rodica and Elena had apparently become bored while folding clothes in the laundry room.

"What happened?" I asked.

"We were just having a little fun riding in the dryer," Rodica replied innocently, "and Ionică is making a big fuss about it."

"How could you possibly ride in a dryer?" I asked in astonishment.

"I just backed in," she confessed.

"And I pushed the little switch on the door to make it go around," said Elena.

"But," I asked, "didn't you realize you could have been hurt very badly? Suppose this would have twisted your back or broken your hip."

"I don't know," responded Rodica, "I didn't think about that."

"I'm sorry," said Elena, rubbing her eyes as tears started to come.

"Girls," said Ionică sternly, "I think you need to understand something. If you would have been injured by such foolishness, Nenea Johnny and I could easily have been sent to prison. That is how our government deals with organizations like ours when a child is hurt. We need to give you a proper punishment so you will remember never to do a foolish thing like this again."

The girls both received several whops with a ruler on their disobedient members—Elena on her hands for having pushed the door switch, and Rodica on her backside for having backed into the dryer. The offense was never repeated.

Several weeks later Ida Jane was invited to spend an evening with Silvia. Silvia, being a diabetic, was always conscious of others suffering from the same disease and was packaging a shipment of sugar-free goodies for diabetic children. Ida went to help with the packaging. It gave her an opportunity to practice her Romanian, and besides, she just enjoyed being with Silvia.

As they worked and talked, time slipped by, and Ida was surprised to realize it was past midnight. Bidding Silvia goodnight, she started driving toward the orphanage, which was only several hundred yards up the road. Right at the intersection of Lipoveni Street, where she needed to turn, stood two policemen. One heavyset officer waved his reflective wand for her to pull to the side of the road. She did so immediately, wondering if she had done something wrong.

In a gruff, authoritative manner, the officer demanded her

license. He soon returned it and barked an order that Ida's underdeveloped language skills couldn't quite grasp. He gestured with his wand in the general direction of the orphanage and repeated his command. *Wonderful,* thought Ida. *He is finished with me and is telling me everything is okay, and that I may go.* Just to be sure, as she was pulling away, she glanced in her rearview mirror. Yes, everything was normal and calm.

Ida slowly drove up to the orphanage and parked. As she got out and walked toward the entrance, she heard running footsteps and a man's voice shouting at her. She stood rooted to the spot as an angry policeman came puffing up to her, demanding that she return to the intersection. Now he not only asked for her license, but her passport as well. Ida again handed over her driver's license and attempted to explain that her passport was at her house. Why was the policeman angry when he had told her to leave? Quickly she explained to Dorel, the night watchman, what had occurred. She called me on the intercom and told me that a policeman wanted to see her passport.

I joined Ida and the watchman, and we walked to the intersection, where we met with a very irate police officer. We tried to explain that Ida had only been in Romania several weeks and could understand very little Romanian. Ida made it clear that she thought she had been released to go, but the policeman interrupted.

"I told you to turn onto Lipoveni Street and wait for me there, and you knew that!" he sputtered, obviously insulted. "Instead, you resisted the authority of a police officer and drove off! You think you can get away with that kind of behavior here in Romania, but I know that in your own country they would shoot you!"

At this ridiculous statement, I stepped forward, placed my hand on the officer's shoulder, and said, "Thank you for not shooting my daughter."

With a flourish, the policeman pulled Ida's driver's license from his jacket pocket and, holding it aloft for all to see, said in an overly loud voice, "It will be a long, long time before anyone gets this back!" Then, stuffing it deep into his pocket, he turned his attention to other late night travelers.

Grasping the situation much better than we Americans, Dorel told us to go on home. We left reluctantly, wondering if we would ever feel at home with this culture or language. We also wondered if we would ever see Ida's driver's license again.

We had barely begun recounting this incident to a rather worried Ruth when there was a knock at the door. Startled, I opened the door. *What now?*

To my amazement, there stood Dorel, whom we had left standing at the intersection just minutes before. He stepped inside, smiled, and handed an astonished Ida Jane her driver's license.

"What? How in the world?" she asked. "How were you able to get this from that policeman?"

"How much did you pay him to get that license back?" I asked, more skeptical than my daughter.

"Nothing!" replied Dorel. "I just explained to him that this girl came here with her parents to help care for the orphanage children. I asked him if he really thought she looked like the type of girl who would deliberately run away from a police officer. I told him he should be ashamed of the poor example he is setting. Then, all of a sudden, he reached into his pocket, handed me your license, and told me to give it back to you."

"Oh, thank you, Dorel! Thank you so very much for helping me out of a difficult situation!" Ida said as she tucked her precious license safely back into her purse.

The living room of the orphanage was understandably large. Among its furnishings were three sofas and several overstuffed chairs. One of the sofas was a 'round-the-corner' type, a favorite among the children. The furniture had just come through a major overhaul to repair the torn covers and replace dislocated springs. It had seen rather rough usage, but was now nicely repaired.

Having noticed some of the children using the furniture for improvised trampolines, I thought this would be a good time to teach the children a lesson on taking better care of the blessings God has given us. With this in mind, I gave strict orders that jumping on the furniture would not be tolerated. "And," I added, "should you forget, I will be on hand to remind you with a punishment so you will remember in the future."

As time went on, several "reminders" were meted out, but we were making progress.

I was striding toward my office one day when, glancing toward the living room, I saw three little girls lined up with their backs toward me. The tinkling sound of their giggles was pleasing to my heart. Just then one of them said, "Go!" In a flash, they took off running.

Wondering just where they could be headed in such a hurry, I dashed into the living room just in time to witness all three of them leaping through the air and landing on the freshly repaired corner sofa. Then, bouncing over its back, they landed in a heap amid gales of laughter.

This was too much! I marched over and retrieved them from behind the sofa, administering a one-smack reminder to each backside. I then explained, "This is no way to treat furniture, and we will have no more of it!"

Each of my three little girls shed a few tears at this reprimand. However, as I continued talking with them, they dried their tears, and I gave them each a hug to let them know I was not angry. Two responded warmly. But one gave me the stiff-shouldered I'm-mad-at-you treatment. Vasilica's sweet little six-year-old face turned into a resolute pout as I again explained that her actions were not acceptable. I reminded her of the rule we had made to keep our furniture looking nice. Her frown only deepened, and she deliberately turned her back on me as I tried to reason with her.

I thought it best to take her into my office, away from prying eyes, to deal further with her obstinate attitude. Closing the office door, I explained that pouting was not going to be tolerated, and that she must stop immediately. She turned her face to the wall and refused to look at me. That did it! I was going to show this little girl just who was boss! I was not going to allow her to get away with this kind of disrespect.

Then a thought flashed into my mind. This little girl had watched in terror as her father brutally mistreated her mother, bringing about her untimely death. Now a man had disciplined her, no doubt awakening memories hidden deep in her heart.

With these thoughts guiding my actions, I tempered the note of authority in my voice with compassion. I gently turned her face from the wall until she was facing me. When her eyes met mine, I said, "I have two beautiful little girls. One is Caroline. And you, Vasilica, are the second one. I cannot let any of my daughters mar the beauty of their character by allowing them to pout when they cannot have their own way." Vasilica's eyes flickered for a moment, then glanced guiltily downward, then she burst into tears. I scooped her up and held her on my lap in silence until she had cried herself out. Then I cupped her little face in my hands, and in my best Romanian said, "I love you." I repeated it again just to make sure she understood. "Vasilica," I asked, "do you believe that I love you?"

She returned my gaze questioningly at first, but then I was rewarded with a most beautiful smile. It began faintly at the corners of her mouth, then spread slowly over her entire face as she softly whispered, *"Da"* (yes). We talked a bit longer and prayed together before she went on her way.

"Come in! Please sit down," I invited Ionică as he entered my office. "How are things?" I asked, though I couldn't help noticing the troubled look on his face.

"Well," he began as he pulled his chair closer to my desk, "I've been wanting to talk to you about David."

David had been the very first child to officially enter the orphanage. His mother had died when he was quite young, and the task of raising so tiny a son had looked impossible to his father. Upon hearing that Americans were opening a new orphanage in Suceava, his father had brought four-year-old David to live with us. He had been a model child from the day he arrived. That had been five years ago, and he was now a strong, robust nine-year-old.

"Let me explain," said Ionică. "There is a strong tradition here in Romania that you must understand. When a child lives in an orphanage, he is usually granted several weeks during the holidays to spend with relatives. This all sounds well and good. The Child Protection Agency promotes the idea. But we have found it just doesn't work out so well."

"Why not?" I asked, wondering how this applied to David.

"Well, during the first several years," continued Ionică, "David rarely went to visit his father. He was mild-tempered, easily trained, and really a delightful child. However, he often talked about his home, his father, and his father's horses. As he grew older, he had a growing desire to visit home more frequently and to stay longer. Last year, at his father's insistence, we let him stay two weeks.

"When David returned, he was a troubled young lad. He climbed out of the van that brought him back and ran straight up to his little bedroom, where he threw himself onto his bed. He lay there, crying 'I don't want to go to hell! I don't want to go to hell!' over and over. It took some probing before we were finally able to discover that David's father had introduced him to alcohol. What else happened to David while he was at home we can only guess. However, we have witnessed firsthand the adverse effects this has had on his normally good behavior. Ever since that visit, David has been more aggressive and has had to be disciplined often.

"Just yesterday," Ionică continued, "when David's third-grade teacher asked him to come up to the board to work a math problem, he rudely declared before the entire class, 'I don't want to!' He refused his teacher's coaxing and pleading, much to the delight of the other students. The teacher was mortified. By the time I found out about the situation, she was in tears, and the classroom was in disorder."

"What did you do about this?" I asked, hoping to get some ideas for dealing with future situations.

"Well, I took him into my office and had a long talk with him," said Ionică. "We are not about to allow a nine-year-old child to disrupt a classroom like that. I gave him an option—either go back to his teacher and apologize in front of the entire class, or I would whip him. He chose to apologize, but I fear he is not truly sorry for what he has done. If that is the case," Ionică concluded gravely, "we will see more such problems."

We continued discussing how David's behavior could affect the other children if we let it go unchecked. Ionică then said, "You know, if we could find a horse for the orphanage children, it might help David. He loves his father's horses and often talks about them. It would give him something positive to think about."

"That's a great idea!" I agreed. "And the quicker the better. But it will have to be a very gentle horse."

After agreeing that Ionică should push ahead and find a horse for the children, and for David in particular, we closed our meeting with prayer, committing David and his problems to the God who alone can give us wisdom to handle complex issues.

CHAPTER 4

THE INCREASE

A crowd had gathered in the remote village of Gardesti in northeastern Romania. The people had come from their small, mud brick houses nestled tightly against the hills that formed the backdrop to their village. The procession of hardworking village folk wove its way around the deepest mud holes in the rutted dirt road and came to a stop near a fresh mound of earth.

Several of the men had obviously been drinking. The priest had walked in from the next village, several miles away. His long black robes were bespeckled with mud from the trail. His voice rose and fell as he mournfully chanted Psalms 23.

Standing on the fringe of the crowd were three elderly women. Their backs were permanently bent from long years of trying to wrest sufficient food from the poor soil to feed their offspring. The center one pointed a gnarled, calloused finger and said to her neighbors, "What's to become of that little boy, Ovidiu? Just think—an orphan at only seven years old." She shook her head as she made a soft clucking noise with her tongue.

"I don't know what's to become of him, but I heard his sisters wanted to care for him," responded a neighbor, shaking her head disapprovingly under the thick black scarf that framed her face.

"It won't work out," said the first. "The oldest one is already sixteen, and she'll be marrying before long."

"I feel so too," said the second. "You don't suppose the evangelicals would take the boy to their orphanage, do you?"

"Now that's a thought," the first lady answered. "His daddy was helping lay the blocks on their church when he took sick and died. I heard he wanted to join that church when it got finished, but he died too soon."

"I don't know if the evangelicals would have let him become a member," said the second woman. "He had a drinking problem, real bad. I think that might have been what caused him to die so young," she continued gravely.

The third lady spoke up. "It's a sin to change the religion you've been born in, and that's what would happen if those evangelicals took the boy. It would be a sin," she declared.

"But," rejoined the first lady, "it'll also be a sin if he stays here. His sisters will be hard put to provide enough for him to eat. And they'll never be able to put him through school, having to buy his books, shoes, and all."

The priest swung his incense burner out over the open grave, which had just received the casket containing the earthly remains of Ovidiu's father.

Standing between his two sisters, Ovidiu watched as blue incense swirled in the afternoon sunshine. Its pungent odor reminded him of his mother's funeral just three months earlier. He felt that hollow feeling deep inside of him again—only this time it was bigger. He was scared. What would happen to him now? Even with his sisters standing beside him, he felt alone.

Taking a shovel, the priest deftly peeled a shovelful of dirt from each of the four sides of the grave, creating an imaginary sign of the cross, as he intoned, "Dust to dust, ashes to ashes. The Lord has given, and the Lord has taken away. Blessed be the name of the Lord."

Villagers drifted away toward their houses as the gravediggers began filling the grave. The priest stepped forward and shook hands with sixteen-year-old Iliana and fourteen-year-old Mona. Then he bent down and shook hands with their little brother Ovidiu. A married brother slipped the priest a small roll of bills, which he placed into the folds of his robe. He acknowledged the giver with a nod and began making his way out of the village and back down the trail leading over the hills.

Months passed, and Ovidiu joined the other village boys as they gathered to watch the new church being completed. He had heard how the CAM assisted evangelist, Nicu Cutlet, had talked with Ovidiu's married brother. He had asked how Ovidiu was doing and whether the family had thought any more about sending Ovidiu to live at the new orphanage in Suceava. But his sisters refused to even consider such a move.

Nearly two years passed. Conditions in Ovidiu's home had become steadily worse. The situation was now almost unbearable. There was never quite enough food to go around, and keeping the house warm during the winter was a constant struggle. The girls toiled endlessly just to keep their clothes clean. Water had to be carried bucket by bucket from the distant village well. The washing was all done by hand. Soap was not only expensive, but had to be carried in over the hills. Under these dire circumstances it was virtually impossible to keep the vermin from their hair and bodies.

Ovidiu's sisters had no mattress. Instead they had collected small saplings from the forest and woven them to fit into an old bed frame. Covering these rough limbs with a blanket, they made do as best they could. It was anything but comfortable, yet they did not complain, for at least they still had each other.

Now it was February, and nine-year-old Ovidiu was helping his sisters work rather than going to school. They still did not have money for clothing and books.

Nicu Cutlet had returned to Ovidiu's village. He was preaching in the newly-built church house just two houses from where Ovidiu lived.

Iliana and Mona talked things over again as they had so many times before. It was a difficult decision, but Iliana realized she just couldn't go on. She sent word to the evangelist to come to their house. Heartbreaking as it was, she was ready to give up Ovidiu and allow him to go live in the Nathaniel Orphanage, where he could have a chance in life. Iliana and Mona gave permission for the evangelist to make the necessary arrangements. After several weeks, all was in order.

"Nenea Johnny, have you seen our new boy yet?" asked Iliuta with a smile as I met him in the orphanage hallway just before breakfast.

"No. What's his name?" I asked.

"His name's Ovidiu, and he's nine years old," responded Iliuta, happy to be the bearer of such good news.

"We were hoping he would come," I said. "When did he arrive?"

"They brought him last night after most of the boys were already in bed."

I lined everyone up then rang the bell for breakfast, but kept an eye out for our new boy.

He had already found his place in the line and flowed right along with the others. I could see that he was shy and would not appreciate being singled out for a formal introduction just then. His reddish-brown hair was most impressive. His ears stuck out prominently, and he had a liberal sprinkling of freckles across his high cheeks and the bridge of his nose. He looked gaunt. His almost-black eyes met mine for just an instant as he marched past on his way to the dining room.

Marian leaned over and whispered to him that we remain standing until we have asked the blessing. Ovidiu gave him a shy smile. His appetite was immense for a boy his size. I was blessed by the thoughtful kindness of the children as they showed him around and looked out for him. I sensed that they were pleased to have him join our family. Now we were fifty-four.

I notified CAM, explaining that Ovidiu Badarau had come and would stay with us pending the legal paperwork and a variance from CAM's policy makers because he exceeded the seven-year-old age limit. We soon received both.

That night as Ruth and I put the children to bed, I felt sorry for Ovidiu as I considered all the adjustments he had to make. I thought about his new experiences fitting in among so many children and learning discipline and order when as a village boy he had done pretty much as he pleased. I went to Pavel's top bunk and told him goodnight. After speaking a bit with Pavel, I moved on to Chip and Ioan. They were brothers who had come from unbelievably poor conditions. I leaned over Chip's bed. His thin arms encircled my neck in an embrace, and I gave him a goodnight kiss. I talked with him several moments, answering his question about what time it was in America where former director Nenea Bill was living, and what he was probably doing just then. As we talked, I glanced toward the foot of Chip's bed and saw a wide forehead and protruding ears silhouetted above the footboard by the light from the open doorway. Very slowly the dark eyes disappeared as the observer lowered himself back onto his pillow. Ovidiu's curiosity had gotten the best of him. He just had to know what this goodnight ritual was all about.

I skipped Ovidiu's bed and told Ioan goodnight. We talked briefly about the new bicycles that were being shipped to the orphanage. He wondered if one of them could be his, and I explained that we had to share them because we had fifty-four children and only ten bicycles.

Last of all I came to Ovidiu's bed. I placed my hand on his shoulder and said, "Goodnight Ovidiu." He made no response. Several evenings later as we continued our ritual Ovidiu responded with a soft, "Goodnight, Nenea Johnny." From then on he seemed to look forward to our short goodnight visits.

We still needed to verify his birth certificate and medical checkups. Then we struggled with how to integrate Ovidiu into our school. He should have started first grade at age seven, but he was nine and had never been to school.

The arrangement between the Romanian government and the Nathaniel Christian School was unique. It was actually a state school, yet we had some control over which teachers would be chosen. We supplied the facilities on our compound and chose our teachers from a pool of state teachers. Originally the school was to be exclusively for the children of the Nathaniel Orphanage. However, early on we made exceptions for little Raluca, the next-door neighbor girl who was from a struggling Christian family. Soon another Christian family from nearby began sending their daughter. Finally our workers' children were included in our student body. The idea of Christian education was being implanted. Ionica became a strong advocate, as did a number of Christian families in our community.

We soon learned that this arrangement with the state would only work through grade four. The state expected all fifth graders to attend state schools. Knowing that these children needed all the help they could get, we looked for ways to keep these children in a Christian school setting. Many of our children had suffered untold abuses in the dysfunctional homes from which they had been rescued. We sought to provide them with the most stable schooling that we possibly could. However, the Romanian school system made a break at the fifth-grade level, and the laws governing fifth-grade students were very stringent.

The Romanian school system was considerably more complex than what we were used to in America. Grades were broken into three groups—grades one through four, five through eight, and nine through twelve. A student's first-grade teacher becomes his second-, third-, and fourth-grade teacher as well. This teacher then cycles back to the first grade and begins to lead another group of students through the first four elementary grades. Teachers qualified for grades one through four must take additional training and pass a battery of tests before becoming qualified to teach grades five through eight. Then more training and tests are required before a teacher can teach grades nine through twelve.

Ovidiu was nine and should have been in third grade. Because of extraordinary Christian teachers we were able to place him in second grade. An experienced teacher took Ovidiu under her wing and tutored him to help him compensate for the schooling he had missed.

The thunder of footsteps rushing pell-mell down the stairs to the accompaniment of excited voices shattered my quiet Saturday morning. Just before the front door of the orphanage banged shut, I heard, "Tata (Daddy) Johnny, he is came, he is came—come queek!" Next I saw girls running down the hallway past my office. They were pulling on sweaters and jackets as they ran. Elena poked her head into my office and beckoned excitedly with her hand. She shouted, "Tata Johnny, come!" then darted after the others.

Grabbing my jacket, I hurried after the children to the little animal barn. An enclosed truck was backing up to the opened barn door. The driver stopped the truck. Ionica got out of the cab and motioned for the children to stand back. He and his helper came to the rear of the truck and carefully opened the large doors. All the children wanted to get a glimpse.

"Children!" shouted Ionica. "If you don't stand back, I'm going to send you into the orphanage right now!" The children grudgingly moved back several paces. The doors were wide open now, and a ramp had been attached. The helper jumped into the back of the truck, and soon the head of a beautiful white mare appeared. The children gasped, and Stella, the long-awaited horse, gave a long introductory whinny. Her ears flicked forward and her nostrils flared as she surveyed her new home.

"Come, horsey," shouted several of the children as they waved their hands in the air.

Stella took a careful step onto the ramp, then another. Then in a rush she bolted all the way down to the barn floor. And there, stumbling along after her, was a dark, two-day-old colt. A whoop of excitement rose from the children, "A baby horse! Tata Johnny, look at the baby horse!" they shouted, smiling at one another in delight.

As soon as the mare and her colt were safely in their stall, the children decided it was time to feed Stella. The gate was lined with children standing shoulder to shoulder, all holding tempting handfuls of hay and extending it through the bars as far as their little arms could stretch. Each hoped that Stella would choose his hay for her breakfast.

"Stella is a wonderful horse, but she has just had a colt, and you must treat her gently," Ionica instructed the children. He went on to explain that the colt had a very good father and should grow up to also be a wonderful horse. "What are you children going to name the little one?" asked Ionica.

"Let's call him Stellutza," suggested one of the children.

"Yes, Stellutza!" chorused the children—and Stellutza it was. This was a good choice, since in Romanian Stella means star, and Stellutza means starlet.

Stellutza proved to be an active little fellow and put on a real show, ducking back and forth under his mother's belly. He paused to nuzzle his mother, nursed several gulps of milk, then ducked back under her belly again. Intrigued, the children sat at the fence and watched for hours.

A week after Stella arrived, Marius came into my office with news.

"Stella is a Christian horse, because a Christian man sold her to us, but her colt is not a Christian, and now we know it."

"How's that?" I asked.

Marius explained, "That sly little Stellutza kicked one of our visitors so hard that she will have to take a bruise back to America with her." As he left my office, I breathed a prayer for the children's protection.

Later that summer Marius worked diligently with the horses, feeding them and cleaning their stalls. He was attempting to separate Stellutza from his mother when, in a split second, the colt whirled and struck out with his hind feet. A sharp little hoof caught Marius on his left temple, cutting completely through the skin and leaving a large U-shaped scar that he would wear for the rest of his life. Stellutza was certainly not showing Christian character!

Marius soon became Stella's trainer, master, and friend. True to his earlier predictions, he galloped Stella all over the farm. He was a born horseman.

Other boys soon followed his example and begged for rides. At first they were led about in the enclosed pasture, but later they were able to ride by themselves. Not to be outdone, Ionela wanted to try riding, and soon other girls stood in line as they waited their turns, pants under their skirts for modesty's sake.

In spite of our hopes that the horse would be a blessing for Timmy, he took very little interest in Stella, but persisted in his bad behavior and belligerent attitude. We did what we could through teaching, training, reprimanding, and disciplining, but all to no avail. It was heartrending to watch helplessly as the life of so promising a boy spun out of control—both his and ours.

CHAPTER 5

CHURCH

The visitors stood outside with me on this beautiful spring Sunday morning. Our gaze took in the church just beyond our little gray house. Across the yet-to-be-planted garden was the farm director's large, two-story house. Alvin and Lil Stoltzfus lived there with their five children, ages nine to twenty. As we watched, the Stoltzfus family emerged and crossed the lawn toward the church.

The mechanic shop and hay storage shed could be seen just below the orchard of young apple trees reaching their slender arms toward the blue spring sky. Beyond that was the barn and dairy complex, complete with cows and milk processing and bottling machines. Twin, two-story, gray buildings dominated the compound. The one nearest the white-fenced roadway was the orphanage; the second was the school and gymnasium.

The sun fully illuminated the orphanage building. The door opened, and a string of twelve girls appeared. They were dressed in their Sunday best and were being led by their daycare worker, Tanti Lanuţa. They chattered merrily among themselves as they walked. Clean concrete walks from the orphanage to the church meant they did not have to dirty their shiny Sunday shoes in the soft, moist earth. The walkway was symbolic of our sincere desire that every child's feet find the path to God and stay on it throughout life.

Before they reached us, another group spilled from the orphanage doorway. It was the boys—all twenty-seven of them—dressed in their white shirts and dark pants. Most were wearing sweaters against the morning chill. They were led by Nenea Geo. Right behind them came the rest of the girls under the watchful eye of Tanti Rodica.

Going to church

American workers from the CAM distribution warehouse in the nearby village of Pătrăuți arrived by car and joined the stream of worshipers entering the church. There were also a number of visitors present, as usual. Many knelt to whisper a silent prayer before taking their seats.

The service began with a Romanian hymn, sung melodiously from hymnals containing only words and no written music. Sunshine poured through the tall windows. I looked about and marveled, realizing that only eight years earlier, under the shadow of communism, such a scene would have been impossible.

The hymn ended, and Willis Bontrager, pastor of the Nathaniel Christian Church, stood to welcome the worshipers and open the service with a time of prayer and praise. Silvia translated for us. Willis read from the Scriptures, then invited the congregation to stand and individually share in prayer as the Lord directed.

Sunday school was conducted with adults, youth, and children all together in the auditorium. Often the theme was illustrated by an object lesson which the children in particular found fascinating. Nathan Bange taught a lesson on the blessing of developing loyalty in our hearts. First he read from the Bible, then he told a story of two youths whose loyalty to each other actually saved their lives. Near the end of the story he drew from his pocket eleven large-headed nails. Ten of these he arranged with their heads interlocking to form an A, then he carefully hung them over the last spike, which he held horizontally. To our amazement they balanced there, each holding up its neighbor. Nathan explained how much we need the loyalty of our Christian brothers and sisters, then looked around and asked, "Could I have a volunteer?"

Hands went up, and Nathan chose Ionela.

"I want you to carefully remove one of these nails without causing another one to fall," Nathan instructed.

The audience sat forward, and the children craned their necks to get a better view. Ionela gingerly maneuvered one nail from among the others. Suddenly the whole arrangement collapsed. Each nail had been dependent upon its neighbor for the interlocking action that held them together. Nathan concluded his lesson by explaining how important it is for us to uphold one another with Christian loyalty.

Following Sunday school, a class of twelve orphanage children gave a short program. Their childish voices touched our hearts as they sang enthusiastically. They then recited a lengthy poem about God awakening the earth with springtime, each child contributing a verse. After another song they took their seats, leaving a trio of nine-year-olds to sing the final song.

Short, chubby Roxana trilled a bell-like soprano while tall, thin Florica supplied a high tenor and Mihaela blended her low, rich alto. Their voices harmonized perfectly as they glanced at a handwritten copy. Where had they learned to sing so well? Maybe it was a natural inclination to sing, born of the Romanians' love for music. Or maybe it was because singing was very much a part of orphanage life, thanks to their tantis, who taught them many songs and a deep appreciation for singing.

A visiting brother sent a note to our pastor asking if he might share a poem, and permission was granted. It was fully twenty minutes later when our visitor finally returned to his seat and our now-wiser pastor was able to give a very condensed version of the sermon he had prepared. Poems are widely used in church services throughout Romania. Lengthy poems are committed to memory, and their flawless recitation is highly esteemed. Developing the memory is a top priority in Romanian schools, and churches benefit from this exercise.

Following the message and dismissal, the worshipers were ready to fellowship with one another. However, this is not the common practice in most Romanian evangelical churches, where one finds it nearly impossible to stand in the middle aisle after dismissal. A continual, aisle-wide flow of worshipers moves steadily toward the main entrance until the church is empty. The Romanian culture holds a deep reverence for the place of worship, and many feel that talking overmuch with friends within the house of prayer does not show due respect. Thus it is common to find worshipers fellowshipping outside, often standing in the snow during the cold winter rather than visiting in the building.

Of the fifty-four children now under our care, few had had the privilege of attending church before coming to the Nathaniel Christian Orphanage. This made for some rather interesting training experiences in their church life.

We were soon to discover that the power of suggestion was alive and well among us. When one little girl needed to use the restroom during a church service, at least six others on her bench soon heeded a similar call. This phenomenon was in no way limited to the girls' side of the house. The disruption and constant flow of children to and fro was totally out of hand, and Ruth finally suggested we do something about it.

So it was decreed that each and every child must use the restroom *before* heading for church, and that going out during the service would be reserved for absolute emergencies—and that by permission only. It seemed so simple to lay down the law, but implementing it proved to be considerably more difficult.

One Sunday, one of our ten-year-old boys turned in his seat and whispered, "Nenea Johnny, I have to go to the bathroom."

"Wait until after church," I replied, and refocused my thoughts on the message. But out of the corner of my eye I kept watching him. He couldn't sit still and kept squirming in his seat. *Maybe his need is real and not imaginary,* I thought. I waited and watched. After ten minutes he turned and again pleaded his case.

"Didn't you use the restroom before coming to church like you were told?" I asked.

"No, I forgot," was his pleading response.

How will I ever teach responsibility to this group of children? I wondered.

"Well," I said, weighing my words carefully as I whispered in his ear, "I'll tell you what I'll do. If you really need to go, you may, but . . ."

"Okay!" he interjected and started to his feet.

"Wait a minute," I continued. "You may go if you must, but tomorrow you will have to wash the dishes as a reminder that you must be responsible to use the restroom *before* coming to church." He sat back down and contemplated this new, unanticipated cost. After several minutes, having made up his mind that wisdom was the better part of valor, he rose and left the sanctuary.

I learned that peeping during prayer was a must if I was to maintain control over the boys under my care. One day I had to give a snap reminder to Gheorghe that prayer is not an opportunity to pester a neighbor on the next bench. Several minutes later I had to manually close Davucu's eyes for the second time, only to hear the sound of whispering coming from a different quarter. Uninterrupted prayer, I learned, was a goal worthy of achieving, but we certainly were not there yet.

Ionică, though a pastor in his own church, visited ours often enough to understand our behavior issues. He was determined to

Church training in the orphanage living room

help teach the children to sit still and listen during church services. One day he commanded all of the benches to be brought from the dining room and set up in the orphanage living room. He had all of the children sit there facing him. "Listen," he cautioned them. "I want you to sit still. No moving about. No wiggling or fidgeting. No whispering. This will be 'practice church,' and I want you to learn reverence."

Tanti Valentina started a song, and the children chimed in lustily. All went well until the third verse, when Ionică's sharp eyes caught a whisperer on the sixth bench. He strode over to the offender and led him to the front of the room, where he made him face the audience. We sang another song, and a daydreamer was led to stand in the ranks of the accused. Ionică read from a passage of Scripture. He progressed verse by verse. Without missing a word or removing his eyes from the page, he walked to a wiggling offender and led her forth to join the swelling crowd at the front of the room.

Ruth capitalized on these methods. She noted the names of girls she saw in church gawking about during prayer. After lunch they were invited to a training session in the privacy of the office. Behind closed doors she lectured them on the value of praying with eyes closed and the need to concentrate on what is being prayed. She explained that prayer is talking with God, and that we need to shut everything else out of our minds and concentrate only on Him. "It is irreverent," she declared, "to open one's eyes and glance about during prayer."

Then she had them kneel and face her. Ruth explained that she was going to keep a watchful eye upon them and asked them to keep their eyes completely closed for a full five minutes. Those who were successful were dismissed with an admonition to pray to God with more reverence in the future. Those who were not successful were invited to stay for a second round of the exercise. A few needed a third dose.

Ruth also dealt with the going-out-during-church syndrome among the girls. She purposely had Roxana and Beti sit next to her in order to help them become more reverent during Sunday evening services.

Brother Bill Mullet had returned for a visit and was preaching a challenging message on sitting together in heavenly places. Ruth was drinking in the message when she noticed that four girls near the front had eluded their tantis and slipped out quietly. Within minutes several others were desperate to go. One of those was Beti, who was sitting near Ruth. She had asked Roxana to make her request known to Ruth. Roxana did her best, but Ruth was absorbed in more heavenly things at the moment. She gave a warning glance in their direction and motioned with her hand for the girls to settle down and be quiet. Roxana tried again, with the same result.

Ruth soon noticed that the girls were creating a commotion. She turned to reprimand them and witnessed, to her amazement, Roxana twisting great folds of her skirt together as though she were wringing water out of it. She repeated this gesture several times until she captured Ruth's undivided attention. Then, pointing to the floor beneath the bench, Roxana showed Ruth the validity of Beti's claim. Ruth was most embarrassed and not only gave them permission to leave, but personally escorted them out.

In spite of all these trials, we did make progress with the children's church decorum.

Six-year-old Beti flounced into my office one day, thrust a Bible into my hands, and announced, "Here, I'm ready to say my verses." She sat down and hitched herself toward the back of the chair. She was so small that her feet dangled several inches above the floor. I took the Bible and noticed that it was opened to the first chapter of Hebrews.

To encourage memorization, the Nathaniel Church had offered a new Bible with a zippered cover to anyone who could stand in front of the church and quote the first two chapters of Hebrews from memory. The orphanage children immediately went to work memorizing these chapters. Many earned their first Bibles this way.

"Okay," I said, "let's see what you can do."

Beti began. "God, who in sundry times, and in divers manners spake in times past to the, to the . . . uh prophets . . ."

"No, Beti," I interrupted. "Spake in times past unto the fathers . . ."

"Oh yes," said Beti, ". . . spake in times past unto the fathers by the prophets, hath in these last days spoken to us by his Son, whom he hath appointed heir over all things, and . . . uh . . . he made the world."

"Let me help you a little bit here," I said, "you didn't get that last part quite right. 'Whom he hath appointed heir over all things, by whom . . .' "

"I know, I know," interjected Beti, ". . . by whom, by whom, uh, also he made the worlds," she finished triumphantly. "Now, may I have my Bible, Tata Johnny, the one with the zipper?"

"Oh, Beti, I don't think you understood correctly," I ventured, feeling sorry for her.

"Yes, you said anyone who says Hebrews one and two will get a Bible with a zipper cover, and I said it," she concluded matter-of-factly.

"But, Beti, look at this," I said, pointing to the open Bible. "True, you said Hebrews chapter one, *verses* one and two, but to receive a Bible you must say all of this." I ran my fingers over Hebrews *chapters* one and two. "See," I continued, "there are a total of thirty-two verses in these chapters, and you have only memorized two of them. I'm sorry, but I can't give you that

Bible yet. But if you will learn the rest of these chapters, I will be glad to give you a Bible."

"Hmm," said Beti, a bit subdued. Then, "Okay, I'll do it. But do I have to say it all at one time?" she asked.

"Well, if it's easier for you to say it one chapter at a time, I'll give you that privilege," I agreed. "But, Beti, who helped you learn these verses that you just quoted?"

"I did," was her prompt reply.

"What do you mean, you did?" I asked. "You don't even go to school yet. Someone had to read those verses for you so you could learn them. Who helped you?"

"No, really!" insisted Beti. "I read them to myself. I learned them all by myself."

I needed proof, so I flipped the Bible she had given me to the following page and said, "Here, read this."

Beti came close and, squinting at the Bible, slowly sounded out the words, "For—the—word—of—God—is—quick—and—powerful . . ." She *read* the entire verse, but I was still not convinced. That was a well-known verse, and she had no doubt memorized it. Flipping to yet another page, I pointed to a verse. "Can you read this one?"

A thrill went through me as I heard Beti sounding out, "That—ye—be—not—slothful—but—followers—of—them—who—through—faith—and—patience—inherit—the—promises." She finished with a glance at me that clearly said, "So there!"

I was absolutely astounded. "But who has been teaching you?" I asked incredulously.

"No one," responded Beti emphatically. "I taught myself."

And she really had. The daycare workers told Ruth that often after lights-out, when everyone else was in bed, they would see Beti holding her Bible to catch the light from the hallway. She pored over it, whispering words under her breath as she taught herself to read. I wanted to give her a Bible then and there, but thought I'd better allow her to earn it.

Two weeks passed. Then one Sunday evening a note was carried up to the minister in charge. At a break in the program he stood and said, "Beti would like to say Hebrews chapter one in front of the church tonight. Beti, you may come forward."

Beti's short little legs carried her gracefully forward to stand before the pulpit, where she turned and faced the audience. She stepped close to the mike, which had been lowered to match her

Beti and her Bible

height, and, taking a deep breath, began. Speaking rapidly, as if racing some unseen challenger, Beti's low voice quoted all fourteen verses of Hebrews chapter one.

Two weeks later, Beti again sent a note, and once more stood before the audience. This time she quoted Hebrews chapter two. I listened to every word as she spoke them, and when she said the last verse, I had to suppress the urge to applaud.

That evening when Beti returned to the orphanage she was wearing a little larger smile than usual, and tucked securely under her pudgy little arm was a nice new Bible with a zippered cover. And I knew beyond any doubt that it was a Bible she could read.

CHAPTER 6

SOWING SEEDS

Early spring came, and the changing weather inspired in me the urge to plant. After garnering numerous used Styrofoam cups following a carry-in lunch, I headed for the bakery storage garage and invited the children to follow. Leon and Iliuţă became my right-hand men as they sifted soil through wire mesh and mixed it with sand. Several girls kept busy filling cups with the finished product. They asked many questions as we worked together.

"Tata Johnny, why are you planting the seeds now? Isn't it too cold?" asked Laura as she filled another cup.

"We have to begin now, even though it's still too cold to plant outside," I explained. "We'll keep them inside, and in seven or eight weeks these tomato plants will be large enough to set out in our garden. By then it should be warm."

"What are you going to do with those trays?" asked Ovidiu, who watched silently from the sidelines.

"I'm going to make a mini garden out of them," I said with a smile. "I'll tell you what, why don't you run down to the woodshop and bring me two boards about a foot long?" Ovidiu was gone in a jiffy.

Florica bounced into the garage at that moment. "What are you doing?" she asked.

"We're planting garden," replied several children at once.

"May I help too?" she asked wistfully.

"Sure," I responded. "The others are working with the cups, but I need someone to fill these wooden trays. Can you do that?" I asked.

"Oh, yes," replied Florica as she grabbed a tray and headed over to where the boys were sifting.

"Hey!" shouted Leon. "Get out of here! You're not supposed to take our dirt!"

"Yes, I am," said Florica, her voice rising, "Nenea Johnny told me to!"

"Not until we mix it with sand!" exclaimed Iliuţă importantly.

"Sand!" exclaimed Florica. "Why sand?"

"Hey, children," I said, "everyone stop for a minute and listen. This soil is actually rotted leaves from the forest. It's very rich. Iliuţă and Leon are sifting little sticks and stones out of it as they shake it through their screen. After it has been sifted, they will mix it with sand. This keeps the soil from packing too hard in the cups and allows water to filter down through it. After the plants begin to grow, the sand allows nice, strong roots to develop. Then, when we set them out in the garden, the plants will have a healthy root system to give them a good start."

"I see," said Laura. "Are you going to plant tomatoes in all these cups?"

"No," I answered, "I'm going to start some cucumbers too. Florica," I instructed, "wait to fill all of these trays with soil until Iliuţă and Leon have finished mixing it with sand."

"Tata Johnny, here's the wood you wanted," said Ovidiu as he laid the pieces on the workbench.

"Good," I responded. "Open my toolbox and bring me the hammer, would you please?"

He handed me the hammer, and I showed him how to nail the two pieces together to form a T. Then I handed him a can of nails. Ovidiu took the nails, the hammer, and the pieces of wood off into a corner by himself. Soon I heard pounding. It took him a while, but he brought me the wood as soon as he had securely fastened the two pieces together.

I asked for the tape measure from my toolbox and marked off the cross section of the T in one-inch intervals. Then, handing Ovidiu large-headed nails, I instructed him to drive one into each of the marks. He left, and again there came the sound of pounding.

Turning back to the workbench, I found three trays nicely filled with mixed potting soil. Five empty ones were beside them. Looking about, I asked, "Where's Florica?"

"She saw one of Tippy's puppies crossing the lawn and took off after it," someone answered.

I stepped through the door and looked all about the compound, but I couldn't see Florica anywhere.

I'll have to teach her that when she's given a job to do, it's very important to do it well and to complete it, I thought.

I returned to the group of children hard at work. "What do you want me to do next?" Laura asked. "I have filled all the cups. See?" she pointed.

"Okay," I instructed, "take this pencil and push gently right into the middle of each cup of soil. Then drop two tomato seeds into each hole and cover them with fresh soil."

"But why two seeds?" she asked. "I thought you wanted only one plant per cup."

"That's true," I explained. "But often not every seed will grow, and this is to make sure we get a plant from each cup."

"What will you do if two plants grow in one cup?" was her next question.

"We will just pinch off the weakest and allow the strongest one to grow," I answered. "Isn't this fun? Just wait until the plants begin to grow; then it really becomes interesting."

Ovidiu returned with all the nails pretty much in place. After straightening a few, I showed him how to pull the T gently through the tray of soil. He was delighted to see how it made neat, miniature rows in our tiny garden. Iliuţă came over to watch.

"These are broccoli seeds," I explained as I tore a small opening in a packet. "See?" I said as I passed the packet along the tiny row, tapping it continuously. Just the right amount of tiny seeds dropped into the row. "There," I said as I handed the packet to Iliuţă, "you want to try?"

"Sure," was his ready response, and he was soon having a grand time planting his miniature garden.

I began filling the remainder of the trays. Laura was planting tomato seeds in the cups. Leon was cleaning up the sticks and stones he had helped filter from the forest soil. Ovidiu was making more rows, and several others were watering with Styrofoam cups punched full of nail holes. This is why I had come to Romania— to interact with all these dear children. And I loved it!

My pleasant thoughts were interrupted by Iliuţă's voice.

"No, you can't," he said emphatically. "Nenea Johnny told me to plant this, and it is very particular. Now stop. You're bumping my arm, and that spills out too many seeds."

Florica soon stood at my side.

"Nenea Johnny, you'll let me plant too, won't you?" she pleaded. "You know my name, don't you? Flori means flower, and Florica means little flower, so you see, I am a little flower." She smiled sweetly. "That's why I just love flowers and plants, so you'll let me plant, won't you?" she asked persistently.

"Well," I said after a moment's contemplation, "I think I gave you a job to do, but you walked off before finishing it, didn't you?"

"Well, no—I mean, yes. I didn't really. But you see, Tippy had pups, and they were under the bicycle house and wouldn't come out. Then one came out, and I just had to go hold it for a minute. Oh, Nenea Johnny, he was so cute, and his little nose is wet and cold when it presses against mine. I just had to go, you know."

"Yes, I know, Florica. Will this be the very last time that puppy will ever come out so you can hold him?" I asked.

"Of course not," she giggled. "He already came out again. He likes me. He licks my face and wiggles his tail real fast, and he has a white spot on his tail just like his mom. I think I'll name him Tippy Two. Do you like that?" she asked.

"Florica, Florica, what am I ever going to do with you?" I asked. "Surely it was important for you to go hold the puppy, but when you get big and work for someone else, they will get angry with you if you run off and chase after a puppy instead of doing the job they have asked you to do."

"Oh. I'm sorry I didn't fill all of the trays, but can I plant now?" she asked. "Please, Nenea Johnny? I really like to plant. Please?"

"No," I said carefully. "I had to do the job you were supposed to do. Iliuţă completed his job, and he did it very well. Now he is planting, and it wouldn't be right to take that away from him and give it to you. Next time you must remember to complete your job before leaving."

"Okay," she said, "next time. Bye. I'm going to see if Tippy Two is out."

The mid-week service was an inspiration to all of us. I felt rejuvenated and ready for the rest of the week. Near the end of the service Brother Willis announced from the pulpit, "We have a little time left if there is someone who is ready to say Hebrews one and two." He scanned the audience. No one responded, so he began making closing comments. Then he saw a hand near the front. "Okay, Marinel," he said, "come right on up."

Marinel stepped up to the mike and gazed at the sea of faces filling the church auditorium. He was eight, but small for his age. His serious eyes and shuffling gait betrayed the suffering he had endured before coming to the orphanage.

Marinel's single mother had forced him out of the dilapidated apartment she shared with three of his brothers. At the tender age of four, he had found himself living the harsh life of a street urchin. At an age when most boys were still being cuddled by their mothers, the only thing Marinel had to embrace was cold, bare concrete. The streets were his home, and the sidewalks were too often his bed.

Autumn had come, and with it bone-chilling temperatures. Marinel shivered in his thin clothing. He was grateful when people living near his haunt gave him cast-off clothing to wear or food to eat. Still, he was often cold and hungry.

One bitterly cold winter night he especially felt the bite of the driving wind. His head ached and he felt feverish. He wished he could go home, but that was impossible. He couldn't endure another beating. He thought about going down to the train station. But no, he didn't wanted to risk meeting the big, cruel boys who made life even more miserable for him. *No*, Marinel thought, *I'll just slip into some apartment building and get out of this terrible wind.*

He found an entrance leading to an apartment stairwell and sneaked through the green metal door. It must have once held glass in its opening, but now there was none. A naked bulb clung to some bare wires and fought feebly against the darkness. The smell of stale tobacco smoke irritated his raw throat. He peered up the staircase, which went up four more floors. Three apartment doors opened onto each small landing, but there was no place for Marinel.

Marinel made his way back to the little corner behind the concrete staircase and curled up there. It was numbingly cold, but better than the sidewalks. The locked door near his head led to a utility room, and he hoped no one would need to go there before morning. He didn't want anyone discovering him and chasing him back out into that bitter wind. He shivered in spite of his fever and wondered what would become of him. He would soon be six, and he had already spent more than a year on the streets. Nothing had changed. He was always hungry. He couldn't remember the last time he had actually felt warm and full.

Marinel couldn't stop shivering, and big tears started trickling down his dirt-stained cheeks. Mercifully, he fell asleep.

High up above, Someone was watching—Someone who looked, and loved, and cared.

God the Father honored His word: "When my father and my mother forsake me, then the Lord will take me up" (Psalms 27:10).

A gruff voice broke into Marinel's feverish sleep.

"What are you doing here on a night like this, my boy?" asked the strange voice.

"Please, mister, don't make me go back outside. I won't cause trouble. I just need a place to sleep. I'll leave in the morning. I promise!" Marinel pleaded.

"But where is your home, and why aren't you there?" continued the gruff voice. "Get up and come with me."

"I don't really have a home I can go to," replied Marinel, "and I—oh, please, mister, just let me stay here till morning," he begged.

"No," said the man, taking Marinel firmly by the arm and pulling him upright.

"Ouch!" whimpered Marinel as he scrambled to his feet. He staggered and almost fell, but the man held him fast.

"What's the matter?" asked the man. "Can't you walk?" But this time his tone wasn't so gruff.

"I—I don't know," said Marinel. "My feet are numb, and I can't bend my ankles."

"Here," said the man, "let me help you." Placing his arm around Marinel, he led him toward the green door. But to Marinel's surprise, the man turned before reaching the door and began helping him climb the stairs. Stiffly they went up, step by step. "Where are you taking me?" asked Marinel.

"To my apartment," responded the man.

"Why?" Marinel asked.

"Because I can't let you sleep down there. You'd be frozen by morning. I'm afraid you may have already frozen your feet."

So Marinel slept under a warm blanket that night.

But all of that was behind him. Right now he had two chapters to quote and a Bible to win. He was determined to do his best. As he stood facing the audience in the Nathaniel Christian Church, he paused, looked at the friendly faces before him, and plunged in.

"God, who at sundry times and in divers manners spake in times past unto the fathers by the prophets . . ." *I will win this Bible! I just have to!* He tried to calm his jittery nerves and started in again. *Oh no! I missed a phrase!*

Quickly he corrected himself and went on. Then he seemed to find his pace, and the verses kept coming. Verse after verse he pulled from his memory. They were there, just as he had stored them, like so many sheets of paper in a stack. He certainly hoped they wouldn't get jumbled up. They came out almost without effort. He was glad for all the hours he had practiced saying them to himself.

Then it happened. His mind went blank! The church became very still. Everyone waited. Marinel looked at the floor and began repeating verses silently, backtracking to jar his memory. Several other boys tried to whisper the phrase he needed, but that only confused him as he tried to untangle his thoughts. He felt the blood rush to his face. Should he quit and sit down? No! He had begun, and he would finish!

Then in a flash he had it! "For verily he took not on him the nature of angels; but he took on him the seed of Abraham."

The next verse flowed, and the following, "For in that he himself hath suffered being tempted, he is able to succour them that are tempted." But what came after that? He was blank once more!

"Thank you, Marinel." Marinel turned. Pastor Willis was stepping toward him, hand outstretched, and in the pastor's hand was a beautiful Bible with a black zippered cover. His! He had done it! He had quoted the first two chapters of Hebrews and earned his new Bible!

Marinel stumbled slightly as he stepped down from the platform. Several of the children snickered, but that didn't matter. He had his very own Bible.

Several days later, Alvin Stoltzfus called to ask if he could take Marinel to town with him. Alvin explained that Marinel wanted to visit a friend.

"Sure," I said, "it's fine with me."

As Alvin and Marinel neared the bridge spanning the Suceava River, Marinel spoke up. "Uh, Nenea Alvin, could we pray before we get there?" he asked.

"Oh, I would be glad to," responded Alvin, and he pulled off the road. Together they asked God's guidance upon this venture. Alvin glanced at Marinel and asked, "What do you have there?"

"It's a gift for my friend."

"Are you sure you know where he lives?" Alvin asked.

"Not really," said Marinel. "It's been several years since I was there."

"Well, do you know the name of the street?" asked Alvin.

"Not really. I didn't go to school when I was living on the streets, so I couldn't read the street signs," he explained.

"So how will I know where to take you?" asked Alvin.

"I'll tell you," responded Marinel.

They traveled across town to the area Marinel indicated. After exploring one fruitless area near a hotel, Alvin turned onto a street that led away from the main part of town, still following Marinel's vague directions.

"Turn right here and go slow. I think we need to turn at the next alley." Marinel struggled to remember.

"Here?" asked Alvin.

"No, this doesn't look right after all. It must be the next one," he explained hesitantly, obviously unsure of himself.

"Here, right here, turn!" said Marinel excitedly. "Yeah, yeah," he squealed, "this is the place! I remember!" Alvin had to grin in spite of himself, for Marinel was bouncing up and down with excitement.

"What was the number of the apartment?" asked Alvin. "They all look alike to me."

"I don't know the number," replied Marinel. "But I know we're getting real close."

Suddenly Marinel's long, thin arm shot out, pointing at one of the many doors in an apartment complex. "That's it!" he shouted. "I'm sure that's it!"

Alvin parked off to the side as far as possible, leaving room for other vehicles to pass by on the narrow street. Together he and Marinel walked up to the door. They entered, and Marinel led the way as they mounted the stairs. Were these the same stairs he had climbed three years earlier? Up they went until they reached the third floor. There Marinel hesitated. He reached up and pinched his lower lip, thinking hard, then he said, "This one," as he indicated the second door. They stood before the door, each waiting for the other to make the next move.

Alvin was skeptical. *Suppose the couple has moved away and someone else lives here? Or what if this isn't even the correct apartment building?*

Marinel reached out and knocked on the door. They waited. A young woman soon opened the door.

"Yes, can I help you?" she asked, looking at the unknown man before her. Alvin just stood there. What should he say? Then the lady glanced down at Marinel. She looked again and blinked, then a smile of recognition flashed across her face and she exclaimed, "Marinel! My, how you have grown! You look so different, I hardly knew you. Oh, I can't believe this! You came to visit me! I wish Vasile were at home, but he's away working. Come in, come in!" she said, sweeping the door wide open and motioning for them to enter.

She and Marinel talked rapidly. They had so much to catch up on. Alvin glanced about the room, noticing that it was tidy and clean.

Suddenly Marinel remembered his gift. Without ceremony he said, "See, I brought you a gift. I appreciate so much what you did for me when I didn't have a place to stay. I wanted to bring you a gift." He smiled.

"Oh, thank you!" said the lady as she took the package from his hand. "Should I open it now?" she asked.

Marinel nodded, grinning.

Almost tenderly she broke the Scotch tape loose from the folds of the crude, brown paper wrapping. Gently she opened it and lifted out a new Romanian Bible with a black zippered cover.

"Oh, Marinel!" she cried. "This is a wonderful gift! We will always treasure it, and when we look at this Bible we will think of you!" She bent over and gave Marinel a hug.

They talked a bit longer, but it was soon time to leave, and they said their goodbyes.

As Marinel followed Alvin down the stairs, he felt a tug at his heart. His Bible, his own Bible—the one he had earned . . . He had to admit it tugged at his heart to leave his Bible behind. But there was another feeling—a feeling of warmth that glowed deep inside of him. He had given his best to God and to others.

CHAPTER 7

HREAŢCA

Willis Bontrager called one morning to confirm plans for Ruth and me to accompany them on a trip to the remote village of Hreaţca. Silvia and Martha Esh, a voluntary worker, also planned to go, as well as Ionică and Mihai, an evangelist who felt called to work in the area.

Neli and Bogdan, children in our orphanage, had come from Hreaţca, and we hoped to make contact with their family, as well as another family from the same village who had contacted Ionică several times, asking if we could take one of their children into our orphanage. We planned to research the situation.

Eight adults crammed into a four-wheel-drive Suburban and left in the darkness of early dawn, anticipating a five-hour drive to the Vaslui area. All went well until we turned from the hard-surfaced road and started on the mud track leading over the hills toward Hreaţca. Although there was a solid frozen base deep down, at least four inches of sticky mud coated the surface. We slipped, slithered, and spun our way over the rut-covered trail across the open fields toward the village.

Many of these villages had been established during the communist era to provide living quarters for collective farm workers. Locations were often chosen with the farms' best interests in mind and with little regard for the people's needs. The farther we traveled, the more obvious this became.

"Look," said Willis. "Somebody is coming our way. What should I do? If I get out of the ruts to let them pass, we might be stuck until summer!"

"That's not a car or a truck," his wife Esther said. "It looks more like a horse and a wagon. I think he'll probably move over and allow us to stay on the road."

"What road?" Willis chuckled under his breath as he fought the wheel. He turned on the windshield wipers as the spinning front wheels kept flinging mud onto the windshield.

Willis driving mud-covered Suburban

We jostled and bumped toward the oncoming wagon. It was obvious that someone would have to yield the right of way. The man on the wagon urged his horse out of the ruts and onto the field. There he stopped and stared in wide-eyed wonder at such fools as would attempt to reach this remote village in a motorized vehicle. I'll never forget the puzzled expression on the man's face as he passed by. He sat straight and tall on the hard board seat near the front of his wagon. Then, looking back over his shoulder at the seemingly endless rutted track, he raised his right hand and made the sign of the cross over his chest, as if to say, "God be with you!"

Farther on our Suburban jumped track with its nose aimed at a steep drop-off. We were in a predicament! Our front wheels were in the left rut, our back wheels in the right rut. If we revved the engine trying to get out of the ruts forward, we would be in danger of flying over the brink and crashing into the valley below. However, when we spun in reverse our angle forced us back the way we had come.

Finally, after spinning our way sideways fifty yards, we came to a place where the ruts were not so deep. There we were able to turn all four wheels into their proper ruts. With a sigh of relief, we headed on toward the village. I remembered our prayer asking God's protection at the beginning of this journey.

Through perseverance, much skill on Willis's part, and the protecting hand of God, we finally made it to Hreaţca. Sixty-five small mud-brick houses huddled together to provide living quarters for the farm workers. The narrow mud streets, slick with ice, were lined on either side by board fences. Here and there a free-roaming chicken or pig picked half-heartedly through the debris, largely ignoring our intrusion.

We stopped to visit Neli and Bogdan's family. As we stepped into their combination kitchen/living room/dining room/bedroom, we observed that the conditions were unquestionably poor. The dampness of the mud-brick house with its dirt floor caused the cold to penetrate in spite of the crackling fire in their earthen cook stove. I better understood now why this family had given their little Neli into our care. With her chronic arthritis, she must have suffered terribly from the cold dampness. Even with our warm, dry conditions, good nutrition, and constant medication, Neli still spent whole days in bed with swollen joints, her eyes glazed with pain.

The house was neat and clean, and Neli's mother queenly. I glanced at the tiny window nestled just under the low ceiling, which allowed a small stream of light to enter their home. Once I had asked Bogdan, "What do you want to do when you get big?" Instantly he had responded, "I want to go to my village and put big windows in my house!" Now I understood why.

Mother and Father Parnica couldn't get enough news about their children. "How are they doing? Is the medicine helping Neli? Is she getting good grades in school? And Bogdan was so little. Is he starting to grow? When can they come home for a visit?" They asked these questions with all the loving concern of Christian parents who truly missed their children.

In spite of Willis's many promptings to cut our visit short because we had so many other places to go, we found it hard to tear ourselves away. As we began to walk through the village once more, Neli and Bogdan's family accompanied us through the mud. They gladly helped us locate the family who wanted their child to live in our orphanage.

Although poor by our standards, we found the tiny two-roomed house with its Christian parents and their twelve children to be a place of peace and contentment. The older children were well trained to help care for the younger ones, and all appeared healthy and happy. The children were clean, and their house was warm with a glow that came from more than just the fire in the stove. The mother introduced us to her five-year-old son, who fought back bitter tears of disappointment upon learning that we would not take him then and there to live in our orphanage.

Surely it wouldn't be right to take a child from such a happy Christian home! Although the mother urged us to take her little son with us, we refused, stating that we would discuss it and send word of our decision later. We understood that they wanted their son to have a better opportunity in life, but we weren't sure this was reason enough to place him in an orphanage.

Beyond their house the village of Hreaţca lay on a downward grade, and the homes seemed poorer the lower we went. Some houses had thatched roofs. The primitive outhouses were made of cornstalks, without the luxury of a roof or a seat. I carefully picked my way through the mud and meltwater that flowed freely down the rutted village road, stepping on the islands of ice which stuck above the mud here and there. One misstep would personally acquaint me with the gooey wet of Romanian springtime.

We were met and welcomed by the pastor of the only church in the village. He was congenial and most helpful in answering our questions, and he agreed to accompany us on the rest of our tour. I wanted to do a little exploring since this was my first time in such a village, so I forged ahead of the rest.

As I was passing the remains of a house, I noticed it had no fence, which was highly unusual. Its roof had a large black hole where the thatching had long since rotted through. Someone had made a feeble attempt to place tar paper and tin over a portion of the thatching. Great sections of stucco mortar had fallen from the walls, leaving its bare mud bricks exposed to the winter elements. Rain had washed away much of the mud, leaving straw sticking out. A large hole gaped in the wall where the mud bricks had completely disintegrated. Glassless windows stared vacantly back at me.

I walked on down the street away from the abandoned house, but stopped when I realized the rest of the group had paused in front of it. I looked again at the translucent plastic that covered the upper portion of a doorframe. Through its murky plastic film I made out three small human faces peering back at me. I retraced my steps.

With the pastor in the lead, we sloughed through the mud toward the door, and the faces retreated deeper into the darkness. To our surprise, we found five children, ages eight to sixteen, living alone in that deplorable hut. Looking about, Martha saw that the only edible things in the house were a small bowl of beans and a pint of cooking oil.

When Esther asked them where their parents were, she was met with blank stares. Neighbors soon gathered and helped supply the missing information. The father had abandoned the family for another woman some time earlier. Under the harsh conditions of winter village life, the mother had evidently given up the fight and had abandoned the children two months earlier. No one had heard from her since. The oldest had married and lived in a corner of the house with her new baby. She and her brother struggled to care for their three younger siblings, but there was obviously not enough to go around. The three youngest—Beni, eight; Monica, nine; and Maria, twelve—touched our hearts. What had they done to deserve such harsh realities of life? What would become of them if no one came to their aid?

What would Christian Aid Ministries say if they could see this? I wondered. *Isn't this why we are here in Romania—to reach out to the needy?*

Martha broke into my reverie. "Johnny," she said, "we just have to take these children to our orphanage. We can't let them stay here."

"I've been thinking the same thing," I replied, "but you know CAM's policy. We are not allowed to take in any child over the age of seven. Maybe we could contact the Ohio office and get special permission in this case."

"Oh, but they need help now!" said Martha.

"That they do," I agreed. "But there isn't room to take them even if we had permission. Have you already forgotten the cramped ride here?"

I walked over to where Ionică and Mihai were talking with Willis and the village pastor. The pastor explained, "The twelve-year-old girl, Maria, attends our church services whenever possible, but she hardly has clothing to wear. Once," he continued soberly, "she passed out in church from what appeared to be a lack of food. Neighbors have helped from time to time, but as you can see, they have very little to spare."

Glancing through the open door into their hovel, I saw Silvia sitting on a stool. She looked like a mother hen giving comfort to the suffering little ones nestled closely about her. She was telling them of her own difficult childhood and how she had trusted in God for help. She was encouraging them to do the same. Maria came up to her shyly, as though confessing some fault, and asked if it would be possible for her to get a pair of shoes so she could attend school.

Willis took the pastor aside and gave him money to help the children. They had broken down their board fence for fuel to keep from freezing during the winter. They desperately needed warm clothing and food.

By this time quite a crowd of villagers had gathered, and Esther decided to disburse the medicines, gloves, and socks she had brought along. She opened the back of our Suburban and busied herself opening several boxes. But she was not prepared for the crowd she faced when she turned to give out the items. At first she wondered about her own safety as she tried to bring order out of the chaos. These normally calm villagers were in a frenzy, each thinking that if they didn't push ahead of the others, there would be nothing left for them. Several tried to trick Esther by hiding the gift they had already received and asking for more as though they had received nothing. The rest of us came to her rescue and decided it would be best if we started back the way we had come. The pastor explained to the crowd that we had given out everything we had brought for them. With a final goodbye, we piled into the Suburban.

We stopped at a roadside spring where we washed sufficient mud from the windshield, lights, and license plates to keep from being ticketed. Then we headed toward our homes in Suceava. For quite some time silence reigned in the Suburban, everyone absorbed in his own thoughts. It was impossible to get those poor, unloved, suffering children out of our minds. We prayed that God would open doors so we could help them.

Several days after our return I made a plea to CAM's main office in Ohio for permission to receive these abandoned children into our orphanage, asking for an exception to the age rule. I well understood the purpose of this rule—to insure that the child's character is still moldable. The younger the child is when he comes into our care, the more readily he adapts to orphanage life and the easier he is to train. Many have had major negative influences in their early lives that must be overcome so they can lead productive lives. The younger they are when this process is begun, the more readily they are able to overcome their pasts.

We soon received permission from CAM's home office to take in the two youngest of these abandoned children. The next hurdle was to work through the legalities with the local authorities. First there had to be a home inspection and a court order stating that these children were truly abandoned. Next the paperwork would have to be drawn up. Would their mother return? Would the local authorities follow through and allow them to be placed with us?

We were disappointed at not receiving permission to take twelve-year-old Maria into our orphanage, and our hearts bled for her. As we thought and prayed about these children, our hearts were burdened. What would become of them?

CHAPTER 8

GROWTH

One Friday afternoon two men from Pătrăuţi came with a shipment of *Seed of Truth* magazines. They carried the bundles into the gym and stacked them neatly against the wall to await packaging later that evening. Sixty thousand magazines had to be unloaded and stacked by hand.

Ionică and several staff workers were engaged in a ping-pong contest, and the competition was hot. After the Pătrăuţi men finished unloading their truck, they stood watching, fascinated, as the evenly matched teams slugged it out.

Ten-year-old Neli came into the gym and stood watching the game. She was rooting for Nenea Ionică's team because she adored him.

Neli often longed to play, but her rheumatoid arthritis would not allow her to. Though she lived with constant pain, she never tired of watching others play.

This game was great. Ionică's team was ahead, but only by two points. Ionică tried to spike the ball, but it flew off the table, giving the opposing team a point. Then it was his partner's serve, but the ball flew into the net. Now the score was tied, twenty to twenty. Neli glanced at the truck driver and his helper. She could tell they were really into this game too.

The opposing team served a fastball, and Ionică swung, but missed it completely. The score was now twenty-one to twenty. Ionică served beautifully, but Donnie gave a smashing blow, and the ball sailed back across the net so fast that Neli could barely follow it. Ionică tried desperately to get out of the way so his partner could take a swing at it, but he wasn't fast enough, and the game was over. The men whooped with laughter and clapped each other on the back as they congratulated the winning team.

Little Neli took it all in with sad, downcast eyes, disappointed that Nenea Ionică's team had lost.

Still laughing, the truck driver joked, "Ionică, you need to go somewhere and take lessons. You really don't know how to play very well."

Neli was appalled! She simply couldn't allow someone to say such rude things about her hero. She spoke up. "Why do you speak to Nenea Ionică so disrespectfully?" Her stinging rebuke silenced the men's laughter. "Don't you know that he is a *director?*"

"What business is this of yours? You're just a little kid; go on and leave us alone," retorted the truck driver roughly.

"I am not a kid; I am a *girl!* Furthermore, you should not be speaking that way to a *director,*" she replied in clipped tones.

"O Lord, be merciful . . ." exclaimed the truck driver, but that's as far as he got.

The players had ceased their banter, captivated by this new match unfolding before them. Little Neli stood barely four feet tall against this burly truck driver. Her tiny finger pointed straight at him as she said accusingly, "You have just taken the Lord's name in vain, and you should never do that!"

"I was not taking the Lord's name in vain," the man replied, "I was just saying . . ." But Neli cut him off.

"What!" she shouted indignantly. "Do you mean to tell

me you don't even know when you have broken the third commandment?"

"And just what do you know about the third commandment—*little girl?*" he asked, his voice dripping with sarcasm.

Neli, astonished that anyone could be so ignorant, stretched herself to her full height and said, "If you can't even remember the third commandment, then you'd better take some lecithin to help your memory!" She gave him a pert nod as she marched off with her head held high.

The ping-pong contestants watched her go, trying to hide their smiles. Neli was so tiny, yet so serious.

The truck driver soon found an excuse to head back to Pătrăuţi, no doubt a bit wiser after his encounter with little Neli.

Over in the bakery garage I continued watering the seed trays and cups and watched for the first appearance of life. I had rigged a bank of fluorescent lights under a plastic canopy to encourage growth. The children were quite interested in our seed project and came running whenever they saw me headed for the bakery garage.

"Are the plants up yet?" they asked every time I went out to water our improvised greenhouse. "Are they up yet, Nenea Johnny? Let me see."

There's something healthy and natural about watching plants grow. When a child's own hands have helped plant and water those seeds, he feels a sense of fulfillment and an underlying awe of God's creative power as they grow and later produce fruit. We may plant and we may water, but, whether the seeds are tomatoes and cucumbers or love and truth, it is God who gives the increase.

"What do you have in those boxes?" asked Roxana as she entered my office.

"Something you've never seen before," was my teasing response.

"What is it?" chimed in Lavinia, who came in right behind her. "Come on, Nenea Johnny, please tell us!" she begged.

"As soon as supper's over, come with me to the bakery garage, and I'll show you what it is," I promised.

"Just tell us now!" they begged.

"I'll give you a hint. It's something that produces food."

"Food?" they repeated in unison as they looked at each other wonderingly.

"Can we cook with it?" asked Loredana as she stood listening from the open doorway.

"No," I responded with a chuckle, "but it does produce heat. Now that's all I'm going to tell you until after we've eaten. Go wash up for supper."

The girls scampered down the hall, still discussing the mysterious boxes.

Supper was soon over, and I was bombarded by no less than eight very curious children.

"Okay, let's go," I said. We carried the boxes to the bakery garage, where eager little hands were ready to help open them. Finally there emerged two blue, plastic, octagon-shaped boxes.

"What is it?" chorused a number of voices together.

"It's an incubator for hatching chicks," I explained.

"You mean we just put eggs into that machine, and it will make chicks?" asked Roxana.

"No," I laughed, "it's not quite that simple. We will place special hatching eggs onto this plastic grid. Then we'll put a little water in the bottom for proper moisture and plug it in. This is the heating element, and here is the thermostat," I explained as I pointed out the components.

"What's a thermostat?" asked Beti.

"The thermostat keeps the eggs from getting too hot or too

cold," I continued. "We want the incubator to keep the eggs the same temperature as a mother hen would. Oh, and another thing—mother hens roll their eggs over several times each day."

"But you can't do that," said Lavinia.

"We must if we want the chicks to hatch," I said.

Elena asked, "What's the airplane propeller for?"

"This fan," I explained, "is to circulate the air evenly around the eggs so all of them receive the same amount of warmth. See?" I demonstrated as I plugged it in and blew air into their upturned faces.

"But where will you get the special eggs for hatching?" asked Ovidiu.

I explained that Vali, our cashier and translator, was checking with a company that produced broiler hatching eggs for commercial growers. He was going to see if they would sell us several dozen eggs for our incubators.

"Tata Johnny, come quick!" The shout came from the other end of the bakery garage. It was Iliuţă. He had lifted a corner of plastic with one hand and was motioning excitedly with the other. I immediately lost my audience as they rushed en masse toward where Iliuţă was standing. He turned to me with a wide grin.

"Tata Johnny," he announced excitedly, "my rows are growing!"

"Where? Where? We want to see too!" said several voices as they pushed against each other for a better view. In due time each was able to get a look, and sure enough, those tiny rows that Iliuţă had planted were green with newly emerged broccoli. I picked up several cups to show the children that the small bulge of soil right in the center of the cup was a new tomato plant pushing its way toward the light. I uncovered one, and they all crowded around to see. Laura wanted a closer look, since she had planted them.

"But where are the leaves?" she asked.

"What you see here is a folded stem. It will pull the leaves above the soil in a day or two as it grows," I explained, passing the cup around for all to see.

Someone near the door shouted, "Willis is here!" and the children headed for the gym. I watered the plants with Iliuţa's help, tucked the plastic securely into place, put the incubators back into their boxes, and went to help pack *Seed of Truth* magazines.

Most of the children were already working as I entered the gym. Willis and his family had organized teams of children to count out fifty magazines per stack. CAM printed and shipped these free magazines to Romania each month, and it was our responsibility to aid in the distribution. Churches all over Romania had ordered copies for their members, and lists were posted on the tables so each church would get the right amount.

Laura, Roxana, Lavinia, and Ionela started singing. Soon the gym resounded with hymn after hymn as we sang and worked together. Boys were kept busy ferrying magazines to the tables, where others filled orders and packed them into boxes. Other children took the packaged boxes to be sorted by address. In less than three hours, sixty thousand magazines were counted, divided, and packaged for easy pickup and distribution.

Willis's wife Esther cleared one of the tables while we men swept up. She loaded it with brownies and milk, and we snacked as we talked. This was a wonderful time for connecting as a staff; the different branches were all together. In one corner was Steve Stoltzfus, a voluntary worker from Pennsylvania, talking with Willis's son Matthew and farm director Alvin. Several of the older orphanage boys were listening in on their farm talk.

Meanwhile, in another corner, Martha, Rose Stoltzfus, and Ida Jane were discussing their difficulties learning Romanian. Suddenly they erupted into laughter, and I couldn't help but eavesdrop to find out what was so funny.

"It's true!" said Ida Jane. "I was working in the laundry when the maintenance man, Donnie, walked in. I wanted to try out a new Romanian word I had been studying, so I said, 'I see you are working with your *cioropi*.' He looked at me blankly, so I repeated, '*cioropi*.'

" 'Excuse me?' he said.

"So I said it again, but this time more slowly and very distinctly. He kept looking at me with a truly perplexed expression. Donnie couldn't find the English words to explain what he thought I was saying, so he demonstrated. He lifted one foot high and bent over, stretching his hands to his raised foot. It looked for all the world like a woman stepping into a pair of hose!

"Then I realized—*cioropi* means stocking. *Ciocan* means hammer. I had used the wrong word!" The others joined her laughter.

"The purchase agent had come to deliver some laundry soap," Ida explained. "He was quite amazed with Donnie's dance! I overheard Donnie telling him about my mistake, and I was terribly embarrassed!"

"Don't worry," chuckled Rose. "You can never learn unless you're willing to make mistakes."

Not far from Ida Jane's group, nine-year-old Ionela was surrounded by a circle of sympathizers examining her new cast. She had slipped while dashing down the stairs, resulting in a chipped bone in her elbow. She walked up with pen in hand and asked me to autograph her cast. I looked it over, but could scarcely find a vacant spot large enough. I reminded her that when Nenea Bill was the director, she had taunted him and run away. He had playfully given chase but had tripped and fallen, breaking his elbow. I asked her, with pen held aloft, if she thought this was God paying her back. She grinned back at me good-naturedly but said she thought it was just because of her own carelessness. I gave her my signature, and she skipped off to her waiting tanti, who was calling the children to get them ready for bed. It was soon time for us to do the same, and folks began heading for home.

A loud shout roused me out of a deep sleep.

"Tata Johnny! Tata Johnny!" came the call over the intercom. "Come queek to the orphanage; come queek!" It was Dorel, our night watchman. I was instantly awake and dressed frantically. *What's wrong?* My mind raced. *It must be something terrible or he never would have called at 2:30 a.m.!* Without pausing to tie my shoes, I raced out the door and glanced toward the orphanage. I was relieved to see no flames at any of the windows. I didn't take the more circuitous route on the dry sidewalks but ran straight through the wet grass in order to gain a few precious seconds. I stuck my hand into my jacket pocket as I ran to make sure the car keys were still there in case I had to make an emergency run to the hospital.

As I neared the orphanage, I could see several people through the window. They were not rushing about, and I wondered if I was already too late. I jerked the door open and rushed in, panting. "What's wrong?"

The night watchman was calmly speaking to Mihai Chibici, an evangelist.

Again I asked, "What's the matter?"

Both men turned toward the short hall just beyond my line of vision. I took a step closer, apprehensive of what I might find. To my utter amazement I saw two small children. The little boy looked back at me, close to tears. But the little girl flashed me a smile of recognition. It was Monica and Beni, the abandoned children we had found in Hreaţca! They had finally come! I rushed to them, knelt down, and put my arms around them both as I welcomed them to our orphanage.

Monica's hair was closely cropped and she looked like a boy. She wore a striped pajama top several sizes too large. A white towel served as a skirt and was held about her waist with a large safety pin. Beni's pants were so small that they stopped just below his knees. Several inches of bare skin showed between his pant legs and the rubber boots he was wearing.

Monica and Beni's welcome at 2:30 a.m.

What a life-changing experience this would be for them! Their new world offered a warm house to live in, plenty of food three times each day, a bathtub, hot and cold running water, a toilet that flushed, and mud-free cemented walkways. What a contrast to the world they had known!

But for now they were exhausted and needed to be washed and put to bed. Our night-duty tanti arrived and took over.

Mihai explained that, while he was preaching in the village of Hreaţca, he had been notified that the children had received their papers and were ready to be transported to the Nathaniel Orphanage. When he returned to Suceava, he was able to bring them along.

I thanked him for his help, bade everyone goodnight, and walked back to my little gray house. Although I was tired, I had too many things on my mind to fall asleep immediately. Monica and Beni were now safe, but what about their twelve-year-old sister, Maria? What would become of her? Would no one care for her needs? How must she feel with her brother and sister gone? With a prayer on my heart I fell into a troubled sleep.

Chapter 9

Plans

Ionică and Vali usually came into my office for our morning conferences. We shared experiences, compared notes, and prayed together. What better way could there be to prepare for the day?

On this particular morning, Ionică asked, "What shall we do with Beni and Monica concerning school? They will soon be nine and ten years old, but neither has had any schooling."

"It seems to me," I said, "that even though this school year is almost over, it would still be good for them to start learning the classroom routine and the discipline of school. That will make it so much easier when they begin school next fall."

Ionică agreed, and we decided to start Monica and Beni in a special beginners' class immediately.

"We have another problem," Ionică said. "David is causing trouble again. His attitude was so good when he first came to us—it's hard to believe this is the same boy.

"I took special interest in David," he continued, "and for a time I took him home with me each evening. I thought I could help him. Some of the other children didn't understand and complained that David was now my only boy. I realized I had to give David less specialized attention and divide my time more evenly among the others. I hoped Stela would help him overcome his resentment toward the orphanage, but his attitude has become worse and worse," he concluded dejectedly.

On one occasion David expressed his destructive character by saying, "I wish a war would come and they would blow this place apart! I'd sure like to help them destroy it!"

I took David into my office. I gently reasoned with him about his wrong attitude, but he took refuge in absolute silence. I tried to appeal to his conscience but received no response. I tried to get him to realize that there was a better side to his nature. I asked him if he didn't want to encourage the good within himself. No response. I appealed to his sense of God and asked him what God must think of his words and actions. I received only stony, unbroken silence for my efforts.

Several weeks later Donnie was smoking sausage in a metal smoker just outside the kitchen when the smoker caught fire. The grease buildup from previous operations created such a cloud of smoke that it engulfed half of the orphanage for several minutes. As we rushed to put out the fire, we stumbled upon David. He was jumping up and down in the thick cloud of smoke shouting, "Oh, goody, goody! The orphanage is going to burn down!"

Monday night came, and with it "Report." As usual, the children gathered in the big living room, and Ionică sat on the large, brown, overstuffed chair. From this position he "held court." Beginning with the older children, each child was called upon to stand as his or her actions for the week were reviewed. Those who had spoken disrespectfully to their tantis were bidden to repent and make restitution. Any who had lied or stolen were strongly reprimanded, and punishments were meted out or privileges withheld according to the offenses.

Ionică knew these children so well that they seldom were able to hide their wrongdoings from him. He was determined to train these children as though they were his own. However, sometimes he missed the mark.

I sat watching the proceedings. Beti, age six, and Ştefi, age five, were asked to stand. Ionică asked them, "Why did you girls ruin the sewing machine by running cardboard through it?"

Beti dropped her head guiltily, but didn't respond. Not so with Ştefi. Typically quiet and gentle, she now held her head high and steadily met Ionică's gaze as she declared, "I did not mess up the sewing machine."

"Where were you?" Ionică demanded. Beti began to sniffle. Several older girls began to titter, and Ionică rebuked them with a withering glare. With order restored, he again turned his attention to the culprits standing before the bar. One of the tantis interrupted by saying, "Ionică, I think it was Ştefania."

"Okay," he responded, "Ştefania, stand with the others."

Reluctantly, Ştefania rose to her feet.

"I said, 'Stand with the others!' " repeated Ionică forcefully. Ştefania moved over to stand beside Beti, her face downcast.

"Now, you girls need to understand something," he declared in his heavy, masculine voice. "The sewing machine is totally off limits. If you touch it, there will be a punishment! Do you hear me? We are not going to let you get by with this. You are not old enough to sew, but you are old enough to know what is yours and what is not. Imagine how you would grow up if we let you just disregard other people's things. Why, you would grow up to be disrespectful of other people and their property, and who wants to be around such a person?"

By this time all three little girls were crying. Beti and Ştefania both had their heads bowed, but not Ştefi. Although tears were streaming down her face, she steadily met Ionică's gaze. Then she sputtered through her tears that she was not guilty.

"Girls," called Ionică, "come to me." Three sniffling girls complied by shuffling up to the chair where Ionică sat.

My mind raced back over the past several weeks, during which Ruth and I had tucked these children into their beds and told them goodnight. We'd had a hard time learning to know little Ştefi because she was so quiet and reserved. Her mother had abandoned the family, leaving her infant daughter in the hospital, and Ştefi's alcoholic father had died before her second birthday, so she had no memory of her parents.

Ştefi had been slow to respond to our affection. One night as Ruth and I bent over her tiny form to tell her goodnight, we had been thrilled when her sober face broke into a slow, gentle smile. She had turned her face to one side and shyly offered her cheek for a goodnight kiss. And one night following a month of these encounters, I had been rewarded when Ştefi's fine-featured hands slipped out from under the covers and encircled my neck. Gazing into my eyes, that shy smile had overspread her serious expression, and she had returned my goodnight kiss. Ruth and I had known then that we were finally accepted into her heart.

But now, fragile little Ştefi stood with the condemned before "Judge Ionică." Was she guilty? We watched and waited. Ştefi held her head high. She waited politely for an opportunity to speak, and when she spoke, it was respectfully.

"Nenea Ionică," she addressed him through her tears, "I did not touch the sewing machine. It was Ştefania, not me." Ştefi spoke without a trace of fear as she gazed up into Ionică's stern face. I realized she was not only innocent, but also indignant at even being questioned. Her pride had definitely been affronted, and she was going to stand her ground.

Glancing at Ionică, I saw the hint of a smile trying to creep over his stern composure. I knew in my heart that little Ştefi had won her case. The adults were feigning yawns and coughs to cover their smiles as Ştefi was told that she might take her seat.

Report was soon over, and the children dismissed. Ionică asked if he could speak with Ruth and me. As the children were getting ready for bed, we sat in the now empty orphanage living room.

"It's about David," he began. "What shall we do with the boy? Several of the children have told me that David has been saying horrible things at school. He has been going around bragging about how he hates God and that if he had a gun he would shoot God. You know, if he were five years old I could pass this off as just childish talk, but he is ten. When I put this together with his defiance in the classroom, his tendency to steal, and his determination to continue in his wrongdoing after we have pleaded and prayed with him, I see this as something quite serious."

Following a lengthy discussion, we came to the conclusion that David would have to be punished for what he had done. Perhaps, Ionică concluded, if it did David no good, at least it would show the other children that this type of behavior was wrong.

As I walked toward my office, I saw Ionică head up the stairs to find David. Later there was a tap at my door, and I invited Ionică to enter. I tried to read the expression on his face and waited for him to tell me what had happened.

Finally he said, "I found David, and I talked with him about this, but I could not punish him. He said he prayed many times to God about this. I asked him if he thinks God forgives him. He said he thinks so."

I looked closely at Ionică and saw tears in his eyes. I recalled that God had given Ionică three daughters, but no sons, and I wondered if this created a special place in his heart for orphaned boys.

Ionică continued, "I didn't punish David this time, but I told him that if he repeats this behavior, next time I will punish him hard."

I, too, was deeply moved, and told Ionică that I entirely supported his decision.

We tried to understand what goes on in the heart of a child like David. He had been so lovable and cooperative when he first came to us. It had seemed he just naturally wanted to be good. But after he had visited his home several times, all of that had changed. Now he only wanted to be with his father. He reacted in bitterness toward those who were trying to help him. In his mind we were the cause for his having been placed in an orphanage. The more often he visited his home, the more unsettled and bitter he became.

The Răducanu brothers, Ioan and Cip, also came from a difficult home situation. They were suffering from malnutrition when we found them. Ionică and Bill Mullet had rescued them and brought them to the orphanage several years earlier. They had been living in filth and squalor, and their parents had been relieved when their sons came to live in our orphanage. Both Ioan and Cip were good boys, well behaved, respectful, and cooperative.

After the boys came to the orphanage, their parents moved all the way to the western part of Romania near the city of Timişoara. The following year they wanted their sons, now ages six and eight, to come spend three weeks of their summer vacation with them. Reluctantly, permission was granted, and their mother came by train to pick them up. She signed papers stating that she would assume legal responsibility for her sons while they were in her care and promised to return them by August 10.

The boys really lived it up. Their parents felt guilty for not being able to provide adequately for their children and for having placed them in an orphanage, so now they gave their sons everything they desired, including the complete freedom to come and go as they pleased. They slept as long as they liked. They swam in the lake as long as they cared to, ate when they wanted, and had no rules. This was really living!

When the time came for them to return, of course the boys

wanted to stay a little longer. Five weeks rolled by, and still the parents had not returned their sons. They had no telephone, so it was impossible for us to call them to find out what had happened. The parents did not contact the orphanage or tell us why they had not returned the boys. We finally sent a representative to bring Ioan and Cip back to Suceava.

By now the boys were no longer accustomed to living with a schedule. They resented having to get up in the morning. They complained when asked to help with small jobs. They had embraced the idea that life outside the orphanage was one big vacation. They spoke in glowing terms of how nice they'd had it while they were gone.

Two weeks passed, and Cip and Ioan seemed to be fitting in a bit better, until one Wednesday evening.

"Are you about ready?" I asked my wife as I glanced out the window. The children were walking rapidly through the drizzle on their way to church.

"Yes," she called pleasantly from the kitchen, where she was preparing supper for the single staff, who had been invited to drop in after the church service.

We were soon settled in church and enjoying the hearty singing pouring forth from the hearts of those gathered for worship. The service progressed with prayer and Scripture reading. I heard shuffling and noisy whispers coming from the vestibule and was surprised to find our watchman, Viorel, talking with a staff member. I joined them as they stepped outside to continue their discussion.

Viorel was quite disturbed, and I soon understood why. He had been told to find Ioan and Cip, since they were not in church. He had come to give his report.

"I looked everywhere," he said. "I checked the bedroom and even looked under the bed—they weren't there. I looked in the kitchen. I went to the farm and looked among the cows. I checked the horse barn, and they are not anywhere!"

The church door opened and ten-year-old Manu stepped out.

"Are you talking about Ioan and Cip?" he asked thoughtfully.

"Yes," I replied, turning toward him. "Do you know where they are?"

"I overheard them talking while I was getting ready for church, and I thought I heard them say they wanted to run away."

"Really?" I asked in surprise. "Did they say where they would go?"

"I thought I heard the word Timişoara," replied Manu, "but since they were whispering, I'm not too sure."

"Thank you, Manu," I said. "Tell Alvin I'm going to help find the boys. Viorel, would you come with me? I'm thinking they might run to their parents. That's a three-hundred-mile journey. If you were a ten-year-old and were planning to run away to a place three hundred miles away, how would you go?" I asked.

"Well," replied Viorel, "I would probably take a train."

"That's exactly what I was thinking. Let's head for the train station." We hopped into the car and lost no time getting to the Iţcani train station.

I was relieved to see that the crowd at the train station was small. If the boys were here, they shouldn't be too hard to find.

Instructing Viorel to go around the left side of the huge station, I walked rapidly around the opposite side, scanning the crowd. But I could not find them. Two trains were sitting on the tracks preparing for departure. I jogged the full length of the first train, looking in the windows for two familiar faces, but I saw none. Then I spied a conductor and told him I was from a nearby orphanage and that we were missing two boys. "They're about this big," I said, indicating their respective heights.

The conductor thought for a moment, but said, "No, I haven't seen any boys like you've described."

I felt sick. What if we could not find them? What if something terrible should happen to them, or we would never hear of them again? Breathing a prayer, I again addressed the conductor, "Sir, do either of these trains leave for Timişoara?"

Again his answer was, "No."

"Thanks!" I blurted over my shoulder as I ran along the remaining train, glancing in each window as I passed. Halfway down the train someone called, "Nenea Johnny!" It was Viorel. He was also searching the train and had walked from the far end, looking in the windows. Frantic, I suggested we look through the crowd once more. Again we split up and worked our way through the people, more slowly and thoroughly this time, but it was futile.

A sign above a window caught my eye. It said, "Information." There were several people in line ahead of me, and I glanced all around, searching while I impatiently waited my turn.

Back at the church, Manu had informed Alvin of our predicament, and Alvin had started a manhunt at the farm while others prayed.

"Yes?" came the voice from the attendant at the window.

"I am looking for two young boys, ages eight and ten," I explained. "They have light sandy hair, but are a bit small for their ages."

"No," replied the woman, shaking her head impatiently before I had even finished my description. "You could ask at the station master's office," she offered as her eyes darted to the next man in line.

With trepidation, I entered the station master's office. He asked in clipped, military fashion what I wanted. Struggling to make my poor Romanian understandable, I explained that I was looking for two young boys from an orphanage. He immediately replied that he hadn't seen any boys of that description and dismissed me.

"Wait a minute," came a pleasant voice from across the room.

Both the stationmaster and I turned toward the voice. It belonged to a kind-faced, middle-aged station secretary. "There were two boys here about that size twenty minutes ago," she said, "but they could not have been from an orphanage because they wore nice clothes. I think they both had matching blue and white coats," she recalled.

"Did they have light, sandy-colored hair?" I asked excitedly.

"I really don't know," she responded thoughtfully. "They had their heads covered with their jacket hoods."

"Tell me, do you know where they were going?" I asked.

"Why, yes," she replied. "They asked if we had a train leaving for Timişoara."

"Did they buy tickets?" I interrupted, stepping closer.

"No. I told them that all trains leaving for Timişoara depart from the Burdujeni station, and they left," she concluded.

"Thank you! Thank you so much!" I exclaimed as I edged toward the door. I had to find Viorel! The Burdujeni train station was four miles away, and we had to get there before the Timişoara train departed. We had already wasted precious minutes, and these boys had a good head start.

I located Viorel and we jumped into the gray Honda. Just as we were leaving we met Alvin, who had left the church service to assist us. I stopped momentarily and explained that the boys had been here, but had left for the Burdujeni station. Alvin indicated that he would follow.

Within minutes we arrived at the large Burdujeni station. I jumped out and shouted instructions to Viorel to head around one way and I would go in the opposite direction. Alvin hadn't yet arrived. To my dismay, I saw that this station was crowded with hundreds of people waiting to make their train connections. It was going to be very difficult to find two little boys in this sea of people. We circled through the crowds, keeping a sharp lookout, but we finally had to admit that we just could not find them.

Viorel and I met at the front entrance of the station to discuss what to do next and were joined by Alvin, Martha, and Pavel, who was Ioan and Cip's roommate.

I was responsible for these children! And I was powerless to find them! I bowed my head and sent a cry of anguish heavenward. "O God," I prayed, "help me—guide me so we can find Ioan and Cip."

We decided to send seekers on four different paths through and around the large station. I cautioned them to go slowly and search thoroughly. "Be sure you don't miss them," I pleaded.

I turned and walked through the crowd toward the tracks. *Left or right?* I wondered. I felt an unexplainable urge to go right. As I stood near the tracks, I turned slowly and allowed my gaze to drift over the huge crowd standing out of the rain under the extended station pavilion. The milling crowd parted for a moment, and at the far end of that human corridor was a small, boyish face staring straight back at me. My heart lurched. Was that Cip? A second later, as the crowd moved and the corridor closed, I thought I glimpsed another face, but I couldn't be sure. Could it be Cip and Ioan? What if they made a run for it? I began walking, not directly through the crowd, but on a circuitous route that would place me nearer those faces. As I walked, I glanced again. The faces hadn't moved. Their eyes were watching my every move. I circled toward the exit on the far side of the station. There the crowd thinned, and I got my first clear look at Ioan and Cip. My heart was pounding. They each had an orphanage bicycle. Would they take off?

I continued moving closer as the tension mounted. Finally I was right in front of them. "Good evening, boys," I said with a show of calmness I certainly didn't feel. I sat down on a park bench behind them.

"Good evening," they murmured without much enthusiasm.

I suppressed the urge to grab Ioan for fear that Cip would

make a run for it. "Where are you going?" I forced myself to ask calmly.

"Home!" said Cip, though it seemed to come out a bit louder that he wanted it to. He was tense.

"Do you have tickets?" I asked. *If I can keep them talking until the others find us, that will make it more difficult for them to get away.*

"Nope," replied Ioan.

"Do you have money for tickets?" I asked.

Both boys shook their heads, "No."

"Then you were just going hop on the train and ride illegally, is that right?" I probed.

"I guess so," murmured Cip, but both of them hung their heads. The teaching they had received on honesty was bothering them.

"And these bicycles you have," I continued, nodding toward the blue bikes they were holding. "These belong to you, right?" I asked.

They shook their heads again, "No."

"Then whose bicycles are they?" I asked.

For a moment they glanced at one another sheepishly, then Cip said, "They belong to the orphanage."

"Oh," I responded as if a new thought had just occurred to me. "You were going to leave the bicycles here at the station for us to pick up, weren't you?"

Cip began to squirm uncomfortably, and Ioan looked as though he wanted to cry.

"Surely you were not going to *steal* these bicycles from the orphanage, were you?" I inquired.

At that moment I heard Viorel saying, "Good evening, Ioan and Cip. What are you doing here?" He stepped closer as I explained about the bikes. I was glad for his support. His being close at hand might further dissuade them from darting away into the crowd.

Viorel asked, "Why did you boys run away like this?"

"Because the daycare worker was mean," said Cip.

"What did he do?" I asked.

"He pinched Ioan's ear, so we're leaving!" he responded emphatically.

"Let me see the ear," I offered.

"Naw," replied Ioan. "It's all right."

I looked up in time to see Alvin, Martha, and Pavel arrive, and the questioning became more intense.

After several minutes I appealed to the boys. "Look," I said, "I understand that you'd rather live with your father and mother instead of at the orphanage. However, there's a right way and a wrong way to go about it, and running away is not the right way. Taking bicycles that do not belong to you is not right either. Let's go back to my house and discuss this. I think Ruth has a good supper fixed for us, and we'll talk about what is the best thing for you to do." *What will I do if they refuse to go with me?* I wondered. *How will this crowd respond if we Americans grab two Romanian boys and manhandle them into our cars?*

I stood and stretched, then reached down and clasped the handlebars of Cip's bicycle. He released it into my grasp. As I pushed it out into the crowd, I called over my shoulder, "Come on." All of my instincts said, "You've got to make sure they are following!" But I didn't look back. I strained my hearing to the uttermost, though, and picked up the beautiful ticking sound of a bicycle being pushed. Bless Pavel's heart! He was right behind me with the other bike. We had arrived at the car and opened the trunk to load them when a car pulled up and Silvia jumped out.

"Where are the boys?" she demanded. "Did you find them?" I jerked my head toward the corner of the train station and said, "I think they're coming."

Silvia took off in the direction I had indicated while I placed the bikes in the open trunk of the Honda. Suddenly Silvia stopped, for around the corner came Alvin, and just behind him Martha, with an arm around each of the boys. She was talking nonstop to them. Behind them came faithful Viorel, watching to make sure everyone got to the car safely. There was no sign of resistance. It looked more like a homecoming. Silvia rushed forward and gave each of the boys a big hug. She began talking Romanian so fast that I couldn't understand a word she said, but the boys loved it. They seemed relieved to be heading back to the orphanage.

Ioan and Cip climbed into the back seat without any prompting. I thought of the children waiting anxiously at the orphanage and of all the questions they would ask when we returned. I suggested that we go on down to the little gray house where Ruth was waiting with supper. Cip said he wasn't hungry, but I insisted that we needed to discuss things.

My sweet wife took it all in stride, as though she usually fixed supper for runaway boys on Wednesday evenings. Following a good meal, we began to talk. I explained that life's problems are often like bad dogs. If we run from our problems, they will chase us the rest of our lives. But if we turn and face our problems squarely, they will tuck their tails between their legs and run away.

"Boys," I said, "you were trying to run away from your troubles, but your troubles would have followed you to Timişoara and throughout your lives. You must learn to face your problems and overcome them."

After a lengthy discussion about their futures, I walked the boys up to their rooms. Ioan and Cip hesitated for a moment, then threw their arms around me and wished me goodnight.

CHAPTER 10

BREAKING THROUGH

Vali obtained some eggs for us from his connection at the broiler farm. However, since the company was not authorized to sell their eggs privately, future deals would have to be conducted under the table.

We weren't comfortable with this arrangement and decided to produce our own broiler breeder flock. A worker returning from America would bring our first generation of hatching eggs.

We already had the first batch of eggs from the hatchery and decided to go ahead and incubate them. A number of fascinated children gathered in the bakery garage to watch me set the eggs.

"Tata Johnny, why are you drawing on the eggs?" asked Costică.

Bending close to show the inquisitive children, I made a thick pencil mark on the egg I was holding. I explained, "God made mother hens with the instinct to turn their eggs several times each day. I will begin with all the marks turned up. When I roll them over, these marks will all be turned down. This way I won't get confused or miss turning some of the eggs."

"How does the mother chicken do it without marks?" asked Leon.

Wow, I thought. *Good question!*

"Leon," I replied, "I really don't know how the mother hen does it, but I know *I* must mark the eggs. If I forget to turn some, the chicks will not develop or hatch properly."

"How many eggs can you put in the incubator?" Loredana asked.

"Fifty, if I'm careful," I responded.

Ten days later I set up a slide projector in the bakery garage. This time, not only the children came to see, but also the workers. I held egg after egg in the bright beam of the projector.

"Look, children," I said, inviting them to come closer, "see the blood veins inside this egg?"

"Where, Tata Johnny?" chorused a number of the children. "We want to see too!"

I tried to give each child ample opportunity to observe as the light shone through the eggshell, but at times the children had to wait on intrigued adults who had also come to see. Seven of the eggs had no life in them, and I set them aside. When I explained that these were not fertile and would not hatch, thrifty Loredana offered to take them to the kitchen for me.

"Since these eggs have been in the incubator for ten days, they won't exactly taste fresh," I explained. "I think we'd best destroy them."

Two brothers, Iliuță and Costică, immediately materialized at my side, their eyes gleaming. "We'll get rid of them for you if you want," they offered.

I smiled as I instructed them to throw them over the fence as far out into the field as they possibly could. Five minutes later they returned. The eggs were gone, but the gleam was still in their eyes. "They exploded very nicely!" Costică exclaimed.

Iliuță asked, "You have more eggs, yes?"

"No," I responded. "Thankfully, it looks as though the rest of them will hatch."

The following week our worker returned from the States and brought with him four dozen hatching eggs from a broiler breeder flock in America. These I marked and placed in the remaining incubator. I hoped to hatch enough parent stock to produce our own hatching eggs in the future.

Winter was reluctant to give way to spring, and by mid-March a thick blanket of snow still covered the ground. Then suddenly the weather began to warm, and soon spring was in full bloom. By this time our broccoli, cabbage, tomato, and pepper plants were ready to be set out. Several of the tomato plants were already setting their first blossoms while root-bound in their cups. The garden soil had been finely tilled and the peas we had planted were already up.

I took a group of children out to the garden. Eager hands transported the plants we had watched grow. Together we made rows in the garden. We dug holes, filled them with water, and transplanted our precious plants from their Styrofoam cups to their more permanent dwellings. The twins, Nicu and Ionuţ, helped drive stakes for the tomatoes under Franklin's direction. It was beautiful to watch the children scampering about the garden like so many lambs frolicking in springtime. They were so eager to help that they sometimes got in our way.

"Nenea Johnny, I want to water the plants, but Oana won't let me," Larisa cried.

"But I was doing it first!" said Oana.

"Here, girls," I called them to me. "Take this bucket to the spigot by the house. Fill it and bring it back. Both of you can help water the plants." I continued digging holes. After a time, I stood and stretched to ease my aching back. I had to smile as I looked about at the happy, contented children all over the garden. There were several places where excited feet had trampled the peas, but I checked my urge to scold. The young peas would recover, but these young children needed this untarnished, memory-forging experience.

Oana and Larisa share a bucket.

"Oh, Tata Johnny!" shouted nine-year-old Ionela as she ran up to me. In her hand was a dejected-looking tomato plant. Its stem was partially broken just below the first branch. "I stepped on it. I'm so sorry! Will it heal?" she asked innocently.

"No," I replied, "it won't heal. But here's another one you can plant in its place." She smiled gratefully as she took it and dashed back toward the empty hole. Her feet made small impressions in the soft soil as she ran. I watched as she wiggled her fingers deep into the muddy hole. She tenderly planted her tomato plant, shook off the mud, and raced on to the next. Watching her made me feel it was just good to be alive.

Over near the little gray house, Ida Jane was on her hands and knees, surrounded by nine sweet little girls all trying to help her dig in the flower bed. They were literally butting heads in their eagerness to plant flowers and line the new flower bed with stones.

I watched, fascinated. It appeared that Oana and Larisa had worked out their differences. Together they maneuvered a bucket of water through the garden, each with one hand on the bucket handle and a perforated cup in the other. A little water sloshed over the rim and wet Larisa's feet. Her spontaneous giggle mingled with the happy chatter I heard all about me. As soon as they arrived at the point where they had left off, they took their cups and together watered the freshly planted tomatoes. They gave the new girl, Monica, a cup and invited her to dip water from the bucket. I loved the way our children were looking out for her and going out of their way to make her feel welcome. No doubt their own memories of loneliness and homesickness made them reach out to comfort Monica.

Monica waters tomatoes.

On school days the children grew tired of being penned up in their classrooms and longed to get outside and enjoy the beautiful warm weather—so much that, in our monthly staff meeting, the daycare workers filed a complaint against the children who had been sneaking outside without completing their homework assignments. Some of the boys had told their tantis they were needed for jobs at the farm or that Tata Johnny wanted them to help in the garden. Others had pretended they'd finished their homework assignments, then stolen quietly away. So a new rule was made to correct this problem. Effective immediately, each child had to allow the daycare worker to examine his homework and sign a pass saying all was completed. Farm, garden, and lawn workers had to see the pass before allowing the child to help with any outside work.

Two days after our staff meeting a trio of girls came dashing across the lawn waving their coveted passes and shouting, "Here, Tata Johnny. Now may I help you work in the garden?"

I examined their passes and handed each of them a hoe. We had barely gotten started when Iosif came with his pass and asked if I didn't think the lawn was tall enough to mow again. Soon he and two other boys were pushing lawn mowers across our expansive lawn.

Ruth thought it was time to plant the beans, so I got things ready. I loaded the hand-pushed seeder with snap bean seed and started out across the garden. CAM's agriculture committee planned to visit our orphanage the next month, so I did my utmost to make the bean rows as straight as possible. Six little boys wanted to assist with the bean planting and walked alongside, each with one hand on the planter to "help" with the steering. So much for straight rows!

That night before going up to tell the children goodnight, I stopped to check the incubators. I heard a feeble "peep, peep" from one of the eggs and picked it up. Silence. Then I gently rocked it back and forth and was rewarded with another "peep" from within the shell. Cradling it in my hands for warmth, I dashed up to the boy's dorm to show Ovidiu and Iliuţă. Every bedroom emptied in less than two minutes. The boys crowded around to listen, but continued to chatter excitedly among themselves so that no one could possibly have heard even if the unhatched chick decided to chirp.

Iliuţă wanted to try. Holding my breath, I allowed him to grasp the egg in his small hands. Of course, his brother Costică begged to hold it next, and then the others all clamored for a turn. Marinel held the egg up to his ear and shook it vigorously.

"No, Marinel," I protested. "You'll kill it! Here, let me show you." I took the egg and, holding it against his ear, gently rocked it from end to end. Suddenly a huge grin lit up his face.

"I heard it! I heard it!" he shouted to the other boys.

"Shhhh, Marinel, not so loud," I cautioned. "This is enough for now. Tomorrow several of you boys can help me build a brooder for the chicks."

"What's a brooder?" asked Manu.

"It's a special pen to keep the chicks warm and protected. I'll show you tomorrow," I promised.

I cupped the precious egg in my hands. "I'm going to put this little chick to bed, and it's time for you to get to bed as well."

"Tata Johnny, are you going to come back to tell us goodnight?" asked Iosif.

"Probably not. I will just tell you goodnight right now."

Iosif hurried over and gave me a big hug. "Thanks for bringing the egg. That was so interesting." His eyes were big. "Goodnight," he said. "And tell Mama Ruth goodnight for me too. Don't forget."

"And Franklin too," added his brother Daniel.

"Yes, tell Franklin goodnight for us," chorused a number of the others.

By this time half of the boys had re-emerged from their rooms. They came by twos and threes to tell me goodnight.

"Look," I finally said, "I have to get this egg back into the incubator. You don't want this chick to die, do you?"

As I eased down the steps, I heard singing coming from the girls' dorm as the tanti concluded their devotions.

I replaced the egg among its brothers and sisters in the warmth of the incubator and hurried down to the little gray house.

"Come on," I said to Ruth, "let's go tell the children goodnight."

"Isn't it too late?" she asked.

"I don't think so," I said. "I already told the boys goodnight, so we'll only go to the girls' dorm."

We went from room to room giving goodnight hugs to the children, thanking them for their help in the garden and giving out general encouragement. Lavinia asked when the chicks were going to hatch, and I told her that by tomorrow evening I thought we would have several chicks. Neli giggled at the thought of the cute little chicks she used to have in her village.

In the third room I sat on the edge of the bed as I had often done before. Beti scooted as far away from me as she could, but kept up a constant chatter all the while. Then, for the first time, Beti crawled over and wiggled into my lap, just for a moment. Then she was off again, standing beside me. "Tata Johnny," she said, "I want you to pray for me." Immediately the girls from the other three beds echoed, "Yes, we want you to pray for us too." Before I could say anything, Larisa, Oana, and Mihaela tumbled out of their beds and knelt beside me.

I looked from one to the other and confessed, "I don't think I'll be able to pray in Romanian, and you won't be able to understand it all."

"That's all right," said Mihaela, and they all nodded in assent.

"Let's all close our eyes, and I will pray."

"Dear Heavenly Father," I prayed. "Tonight as you look down, you see each one of us, and you see our needs. I pray for Larisa. She cannot live with her family. Comfort her heart. Help us to be a family to her. Take the ashes of her tragic past and change them into something beautiful for you.

"I also pray for Oana. Her mother abandoned her when she was just a baby, and she doesn't know where her mother is. I pray that you will send some Christian to witness to her mother that she might come to know you. Oana cannot remember her father either. Help me to be like a father to her. Cut all ties of sin in Oana's past. Fill that emptiness in her heart, and help her to grow up serving you.

"Heavenly Father, I also pray for Mihaela. Her heart aches to be with her other brothers and sisters. Bring emotional and spiritual healing to her father, and bless her with a heart that wants to do right. Be with her grandma and grandpa just now. Bless them for their faithfulness and their love for Mihaela.

"I pray for Beti, who doesn't know either her mother or her father. Lord, you know the problems that existed in her family. I pray that you would erase the ugliness of her past and replace it with the beauty of your holiness. Direct her in life to become more like you.

"And now, Heavenly Father, I ask your protection over us as we rest this night. Refresh us with sleep, and awaken us in the morning to serve you another day. In Jesus' name I pray. Amen."

For a moment all was still, then Beti broke the silence. "Did you hear him? He prayed for me."

"He prayed for me too," said Larisa and Mihaela in unison.

Then Oana spoke up with an air of importance, "But he prayed *longest* for me!" she announced.

I was deep in thought as I headed for home that evening. *How these darling children are starved for love and attention! Lord, help me fill that void.*

The following afternoon I entered the bakery garage to the chirping of newly hatched chicks clamoring to be taken out of the incubator. Several more were still hatching.

I began converting a four-foot by six-foot plywood box into a makeshift brooder for our chick family. Laura entered and asked, "What's that noise?"

"Go lift the lid on the incubator," I prompted as I worked.

She lifted the lid and asked, "Is it true that they sing through their shells, Tata Johnny? Iliuţă told me in school today that he heard a chick singing through the eggshell. Is that really true?"

"Yes, but that's not what you hear now. Lift the lid on the other incubator," I instructed.

"Oh, this one!" she exclaimed. "They're so cute! May I hold one?"

"Sure, if you like. But be careful," I said.

"Ooooh, here's one that is all wet, and he can't walk. What's wrong with him?" asked Laura pathetically.

I looked over her shoulder. There was nothing wrong with the chick except that it had just hatched. I explained that in another thirty minutes it would be dry and fluffy and running about like all the others.

"Do you want to remove that empty shell?" I asked.

Gingerly she reached her hand through the chirping mass of lively chicks, but when she took hold of the empty eggshell, she gasped as her thumb slipped inside. "Yuck!" she said. "It's all wet and bloody!"

I glanced up from my work several minutes later and saw Laura with a chick cuddled in her arms as if it were a baby. The chick was chirping loudly, as lost chicks do, and she was trying to soothe it with loving words. Soon she placed it back among the others and skipped out the door. In her excitement she forgot to place the top back on the incubator. I replaced the lid and resumed my brooder project. Minutes

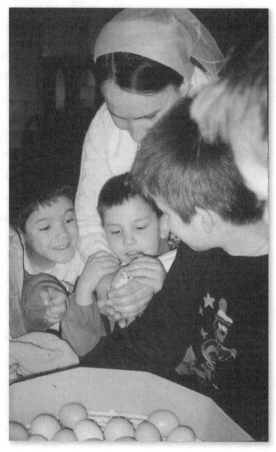

Others watch enviously as Gigi is taught to hold a chick.

later I was interrupted by a group of excited children led by their tanti.

"The children were doing their homework," she exclaimed, "when Laura came in and told them that the chicks had hatched, and that she had held one. Now they all want to hold a chick," she said apologetically. "They can't seem to think about anything else—especially homework."

One by one I captured hapless chicks for each of them to hold and gave strict instructions not to let them fall. Overzealous six-year-old Gigi was squeezing his chick way too hard. I showed him how to hold it gently, and the gleam in his eyes as he cuddled the downy chick to his cheek was well worth the effort. He could well relate to this lonely, chirping chick. He had never known his father or mother either and had spent the first three years of his life in a baby orphanage. His experience there had been somewhat like being in an incubator.

Gigi wanted to help me finish the brooder, and I sent him to the barn to bring me a sack of shavings in the orphanage's little red wagon. Off he went, glad to be of help. I cut two observation windows in our little brooder for the smaller children to see through. Next I rigged up a waterer and feeder. Gigi returned with the shavings and helped me spread them evenly over the floor. Even though the chicks needed to stay in the incubator until the next day, I gave in to Gigi's begging to allow a few to check out their new home. He seemed much more delighted with it than the chicks did, and we soon returned them to their warm incubator.

Several evenings later Ruth and I were again making our rounds through the dorms telling the children goodnight. We finished the boys' side and began with the girls. Lavinia had a lot to talk about with Ruth, so I went on to the next room. I again sat on the edge of Beti's bed, and she scooted toward the wall as usual. Two of the other girls were already asleep, but Beti was in a very talkative mood. She inched a bit closer as I told her a story of when I was a little boy no bigger that she was. Timidly she crawled closer. Then she climbed onto my lap. "Where's Mama Ruth?" she interrupted my story. I explained that I had left her in another room talking with Lavinia. Next she wanted to know about the chicks, and whether any of the American eggs had hatched yet. I told her it would be several more days before they would begin hatching. In an unusual move, Beti reached up and twiddled her chubby little fingers through my beard.

"Why do you have a beard?" she asked.

"Why, Beti," I replied, "God created mature men with beards. Besides, I like to wear a beard because Jesus wore one, and I want to remind others of Jesus."

"How do you know He did?" was her immediate question.

"Well, the Bible says He did," I replied.

In a second she slid off my lap, sprinted across the room and returned with a Bible. Crawling back onto my lap, she thrust the Bible into my hand and said, "Show me." Thoughtfully I opened the Bible, hoping there was a picture of the Good Shepherd in the front. There wasn't. Lamely, I said, "Well, there's a place in the Bible, although I'm not exactly sure where it's found, where it says bad men pulled the hair out of Jesus' cheeks."

"I know," interrupted Beti. "And they blindfolded Him, put a crown of thorns on His head, hit Him, spit on Him, and then they nailed Him to a cross," she said all in one breath.

I was amazed, not only at her knowledge of the Bible, but at how her mind grasped details and arranged them in logical order. I wondered if this girl might someday become a Christian schoolteacher.

Ruth entered and told Beti goodnight. Beti wasn't ready to give us a hug or a kiss, but she was beginning to look forward to our evening visits and talks. We were happy for this small sign of progress. She had been abandoned on the streets of Vaslui at the age of four and had developed a tough, streetwise demeanor and vocabulary which she had brought with her to the Nathaniel Christian Orphanage and often displayed by pushing her way through and pounding other children much larger than herself to get her way. We watched, wondering what God's love was going to accomplish in Beti's life.

CHAPTER 11

LEAVING

The chicks developed wonderfully on Alvin's feed ration, and the boys received firsthand experience down at the farm, where they assisted the hired men in grinding and mixing the feed.

Children constantly peeped through the small observation windows as the little yellow fluff balls scampered about. Occasionally a child would sing out, "Tata Johnny, I saw one trying to fly! He was flapping his wings and running real fast!"

Six-year-old Mariana, with a face that registered deep concern, said, "I think one is sick. I saw him open his mouth real wide like this. Look, Tata Johnny." I had to smile as I watched her imitate the chick's yawn.

Then her sister, Mihaela, shouted from the other observation port, "Tata Johnny, one of the chicks died!" When I looked at her doubtfully, she responded, "Really, it did! Come see!" I bent over and peered at the chick lying on its side under the heat of the brooder lamp. Without saying anything, I reached over the wall of the brooder and nudged the chick with my finger. Instantly it lifted its head and sprang to life, dashing away from my hand so fast that tiny bits of bedding were flung into the air as it ran to join its comrades. I glanced at Mihaela, who gave me a relieved smile and said, "I guess he was just sleeping."

When I noticed how the children loved to watch the chicks through the brooder's observation windows, I got an idea. What if I put windows into the incubator so they could watch the chicks as they hatched? Carefully I fashioned three-inch extensions with observation windows to be placed between the body and the lid of the incubators. We could hardly wait until the next batch started hatching! Periodically I found children with their little noses pressed against the shell of the incubator as they checked for signs of life. Would they never hatch?

"Three, Nenea Johnny, three!" shouted Daniel at the top of his lungs, holding up three fingers for emphasis. He whirled about and glued his wide eyes back to the incubator's window.

At times I feared for the lives of those fluffy little bundles as I watched fifteen overly eager children vying for the four tiny observation ports. They jostled the incubator and each other, bumping heads as several children tried to peer into one small window. I really couldn't blame them. After all, we adults had the same glow on our faces as we witnessed again the wonder of God's creation.

"Nenea Johnny, could I open one?" asked Nicu after it became evident that several eggs were not going to hatch.

"Yes, but take it outside. It might be rotten."

Soon he called me to come and see. I could make out tiny pin-head eyes developed on a pea-sized embryo. Nicu studied the tiny chick in fascination, then left the egg in the grass.

An hour later I saw three girls near the bakery and walked over to investigate. To my surprise I found them sorrowfully holding a vigil over a tenderly constructed grass grave with a little cross made of twigs. I was struck by the tenderness of a child's heart and remembered that the Saviour admonished us to become as little children.

One little chick had hatched with a deformed leg. It was so twisted that it actually stuck up over its head. I was going to kill it so it wouldn't have to suffer, but the children put up such a howl of protest that I chose to let nature take its course. I was sure it couldn't survive long.

This chick captured the hearts of the children as it learned to hop about, competing for its share of food and water. I once caught Beti hanging over the wall of the brooder, in danger of falling headlong among the chicks.

"Beti," I demanded, "what do you think you're doing?"

"I'm catching my chick. I want to hold it," came her ready response.

I watched, and sure enough, when Beti emerged she tenderly held in her hand the one-legged chick.

Several of the boys helped me cut two-by-two framing with which to build four movable chicken pens. Elena and Rodica painted them. Or at least they tried. What paint didn't end up on their hands, their dresses, or the ground did eventually get brushed onto the wood. But this was a learning experience for these ten-year-old girls.

Ovidiu and Iliuţă helped me put the frames together and cover them with chicken wire. As soon as the chicks were old enough, we placed them in these pens on the lawn and in the orchard where plenty of grass was available. We taught the children to care for the broilers by feeding and watering them and moving their pens to fresh locations regularly. There was so much interest in feeding the chicks that the children literally poured it on. I once dug a five-gallon bucket of wasted feed from the brooder bedding. It didn't go to waste. I sent it with Iliuţă for the pigs.

"They liked it very much!" he reported upon his return.

The children showed great interest in the pastured chickens, and I often found them sitting beside one of the pens watching the young chickens as they scratched, ate, and grew.

"Tata Johnny," said Beti one day as she sat watching the broilers, "what are you going to do with these chickens when they get big? Are you going to put them into a chicken house and let them lay eggs?"

"No, Beti," I answered cautiously. "We will butcher these and freeze them. Then this coming winter we can enjoy good-tasting chicken. Won't that be nice?"

"Are you going to butcher the American chickens too?" was her next question.

"No. I'm hoping to save them to lay eggs so we can raise more chicks," I explained tactfully.

"But that's not fair," she protested.

"What's not fair?" asked several girls who had joined her to watch the chicks.

"Tata Johnny said he is going to kill all the Romanian chickens and eat them, but he is going to let the American chickens live, and that's not right!" sputtered Beti. The others were convinced of this injustice and nodded enthusiastically.

Two things made me change my idea about raising the American chicks for a breeder flock. One was the fact that we had a poor hatching ratio from the eggs. The other was the realization that our children would view this as a cultural injustice. We decided it would be best to butcher them all.

I drafted blueprints for butchering funnels, which I submitted to our senior metal worker, Vasile, who fabricated them. Then came butchering day, and we all gathered out behind the barn for the event. All the children were present, as well as most of the workers. The boys brought the broilers to me from their pens, carrying them by their feet. But the girls tenderly carried each broiler in their arms as they would have carried a beloved doll.

The broilers were properly bled in their funnels, then scalded in hot water carried by the big boys from the milk house. As soon as their feathers were sufficiently loosened, all the children wanted to help pluck. I noticed some of the children standing in pairs. One held the hapless broiler by its legs while the other pulled out its white feathers. The plucked feathers soon dried and were blown about by the wind, making the back of the barn area appear as though we had just experienced a summer snowstorm. Alvin and I agreed that there had to be a better way.

Girls tenderly carry the broilers.

When it came to cleaning the entrails from the chickens, I was surprised to find so many willing hands. They all stuck right with me until seventy broilers were ready for the freezer.

On Sunday we all enjoyed fried chicken. There was something special about the children partaking of the fruits of their own labor. I rose to commend them.

"Children," I said once I had their attention, "some of you recall when the chicks first hatched." Heads nodded as they remembered. "Some helped build pens, others mixed feed. Still others helped feed the chickens and move their pens. I'm sure you didn't always feel like continuing your work, but you stuck to your jobs, and now all of us have received a blessing from your labors. I wish to thank all of you, especially for the way you helped with the butchering."

There followed a spontaneous round of applause, not for my speech, but for all those who had labored that we might be blessed. And the chicken was especially good!

Delighted to be part of the work force, Monica, Gabi, Daniela, and Elena eagerly pluck feathers from the orphanage's first broiler flock.

The very next week I drafted plans for a chicken plucker and a scalder to be constructed from fifty-five-gallon drums. Again Vasile came to the rescue with a motor, several feet of pipe, an electrical valve scavenged from a washing machine, and his know-how. Would it work? We could hardly wait until the next batch of broilers to find out.

One Friday I answered the phone. "Nathaniel Christian Orphanage. Good afternoon."

The voice on the other end sounded distant. "I am Cip and Ioan's father. Our sons no longer want to live in the Nathaniel Orphanage. My wife and I have talked this over, and we feel it is best under the circumstances to bring them home to live with us. I plan to come this weekend to get them. Would you please have all the legal papers ready? Thank you," he said, and hung up.

I reported this to Ionică.

"I don't know," said Ionică. "I saw their house. They have nothing—no food, no clothes, nothing for children. But this is their decision."

We agreed that, since these boys wanted so much to be with their parents, we shouldn't fight their desire, but allow them to go. We would reserve their beds for more needy children who had neither father nor mother. Not wanting other children to think they could leave the orphanage and return at will, we agreed that once Ioan and Cip left, we would not receive them back into the orphanage.

On Sunday morning, just before church services were to begin, Cip and Ioan's mother arrived. I met her and invited her to attend the service with us. She seemed very upset and refused to even acknowledge my smile. She did attend the church service, though, and joined us at the orphanage for the noon meal.

After lunch the orphanage administrators met with her and thoroughly discussed the situation. We pointed out that her sons had not really been discipline problems and that we were not forcing them to leave. They were the ones insisting on leaving. As far as we were concerned, they could continue living with us, and we would provide for their needs. However, we didn't want any more talk of running away or encouraging others to do so. We explained that we had heard through other boys that Cip and Ioan had been urging others to join them as they made plans to run away again.

Mrs. Răducanu seemed to understand why we could not take her sons back once they left. She agreed with us that it would be best if they stayed, but was not sure the boys would be willing.

We encouraged Mrs. Răducanu to take time to speak with her sons alone and showed them into our private conference room. There she explained to Cip and Ioan how their lives would be changed if they insisted on leaving the orphanage. She pleaded with her sons to consider the fact that their father, with his failing eyesight, was unable to hold down a job, and that they would be forced to work to support themselves. They would have to go to school in the morning, work to help provide for the family in the afternoon, and study their homework at night. There would be only one meal per day in their home instead of the three they were accustomed to in the orphanage. Winter was coming on, and they would experience cold instead of the cozy central heating of the orphanage.

"Look at the nice clothes you have," she reminded them. "You will soon outgrow them, and I cannot buy you more. What will we do then?"

Following this thorough explanation, she asked her sons many heart-searching questions, but they resolutely refused to answer her and sat in stubborn silence.

Finally Mrs. Răducanu opened the conference room door and announced, "My sons refuse to listen; they insist on leaving."

Ionică went into his office and soon returned with the legal papers. He read them to Mrs. Răducanu and explained that, in the eyes of the Romanian government, she and her husband were resuming full responsibility for Cip and Ioan, and that the Nathaniel Christian Orphanage would no longer be responsible in any way for her sons. "And," he continued, "once they leave, they will no longer be eligible to return as residents of this orphanage." The boys were also informed of these conditions.

News of the Răducanu brothers' imminent departure spread like wildfire through the orphanage compound. Children gathered in the living room and stood shyly about, saying nothing. It was like their brothers were leaving home for good, and they didn't know what to say. Ioan and Cip made feeble attempts at lighthearted talk with several of their closest friends, but their efforts fell flat. Their mother announced that they needed to catch the evening train, and the boys went up to their bedroom with their tanti to gather their clothing. In a short time they returned to the living room, their backpacks stuffed with their belongings. Cip and Ioan acted carefree, as though they were leaving for another vacation, but the soberness of the other children told the true story. They sensed deep within their hearts that this was a permanent parting of ways, a life-changing experience.

Ionică sat alone, looking forlorn. He had personally invested a great deal in these boys' lives. Ioan and Cip hesitated when the time came to walk out to the waiting car. Cip took a step in Ionică's direction, but Ionică shook his head and motioned for them to leave. It seemed harsh to me, but I realized that Ionică just couldn't bear to see these boys return to the life from which he had rescued them. Neither could he bear to tell them goodbye.

They were soon in the gray Honda with their packs of clothing tucked safely into the trunk. The boys sat with their mother in the back, and Martha occupied the passenger's seat. I climbed into the driver's seat, glancing at the orphanage. The doorways and windows were filled with little faces. A few waved sadly as we began to leave. While we were still in the parking lot, I stopped the car and addressed Cip and Ioan one last time.

"Boys," I said, "you think leaving the orphanage is going to make life easier for you, but you are mistaken. Life is harsh, and you will suffer. We have taught you about God and the Bible. We have taught you in school. We have cared for you as our own children. Even now, if you change your minds and decide to stay, I will park this car, and we'll take your clothes back up to your room, and that will be the end of it. If you are still determined to leave, I will take you to the train station. This is your last opportunity to change your minds. Once we leave, I will not turn back. When you pass through that gate you will be on your own, and you can never come back to live at the Nathaniel Christian Orphanage again. You will be welcome to visit anytime, but never to live here. Do you understand?"

Both boys murmured, "Yes."

"Now think this over carefully and give me your answer."

A serious battle was raging in the back seat. Both boys sat with heads bowed. I heard Ioan begin to cry softly. I prayed that my stern warning would break their resolve as I waited breathlessly for their answer. The silence was broken by a whispered exchange. Then ten-year-old Cip announced, "We are leaving!"

"Okay," I said as I put the gray Honda into gear. We rolled through the gate and headed for the train station, riding in sober silence. Just as we arrived at the station, Cip spoke up. "My mom says she doesn't have enough money for our train tickets." Martha and I exchanged glances. Was this an indication of many more experiences to come? I only had a few dollars on me, and Martha didn't have much either. Martha and I emptied our wallets and gave what we had to Mrs. Răducanu and her sons. My heart went out to her. I wondered why her ten-year-old son was allowed to make a decision that would radically affect the future of their entire family. I prayed that God would help them in the coming days.

We stayed at the station until they boarded the train and found their seats. Even then we waited beside the tracks, reluctant to leave. The whistle blew, and the train carrying the Răducanu brothers and their mother began rolling slowly out of the station. Two small heads immediately appeared at a window. I watched, transfixed. Although tears blurred my vision, I saw them waving, and I waved back as the train carried Cip and Ioan farther and farther from our love and care. I continued waving. Their arms waved back from the open train window until they were finally lost from sight. Quietly Martha and I returned to the orphanage, wondering if we would ever see Cip and Ioan again.

That evening I took Ionică to catch the late night train for Cluj, where his four-year-old daughter Iulia was undergoing tests for a heart ailment. Although he was weighed down with the burden of what his own family might face, he said with heartfelt concern, "I wonder where Cip and Ioan are. I hope we see them again . . ."

David's difficulties came up again at a meeting the following week. We hoped the start of school would help refocus his mind on better things. David had seemed less affected and quieter than usual after his most recent visit home. We sincerely hoped this was an indication of better days to come.

As the meeting ended, Ionică turned to me and said, "Johnny, I want you to pray for our four-year-old daughter, Iulia."

"We will pray," I responded. "What have the tests revealed?"

"The doctor says she has a hole in her heart, and we must fix it. Tomorrow night I'm going with my wife and Iulia to Cluj for tests and to meet the surgeons," he explained. "I may be gone for three to five days."

I realized the risk involved and assured him of our concern and our prayers on Iulia's behalf.

At the close of our meeting, we stood and prayed together that God would tenderly care for Iulia and those who would be working with her. The following evening Ionică boarded the train for Cluj with his wife and child. Our hearts and our prayers went with them.

CHAPTER 12

THE TOUR

I was often interrupted while writing my reports by visitors who dropped in unannounced. At times they needed medicines. A month's supply of medications often cost more than the person's whole income. When possible, we helped using CAM's donated medicines. When that was not possible, we often provided help through a local pharmacy. Others came seeking financial help. Still others came out of honest curiosity. They had been told about the Nathaniel Christian Orphanage, and simply wanted to come see for themselves if what they had heard was true.

One day as I sat in my office typing away, Tina stepped in and said, "Tata Johnny, a van load of visitors just arrived."

"How many are there?" I asked.

"I don't know," she replied. "Lots."

I went outside, where a large van was disgorging its road-weary occupants. They stretched as they exited their vehicle like folks who had been traveling for quite some time. Their tall, elderly spokesman introduced himself and explained, "We are from Norway and heard about your orphanage from friends. They told us to be sure and stop in when we came to Romania, so here we are." His accent was thick, but his smile was genuine. He went on to explain that they were Christians and wanted to visit our facilities and hear about our programs.

"Sure!" I smiled in welcome. "Come right on in and I'll show you around." There were thirteen in all, and they formed a semi-circle around me as we gathered in the spacious orphanage living room. I asked if they could all speak English, and the spokesman informed me that nearly half of them could understand it, and that he could interpret for the others, but would I please speak slowly.

"Of course," I said. "Please, everyone find seats, and let me tell you about our orphanage. I will tell you how it began and explain our vision and goals." I shook hands with several of the visitors and introduced myself as they found their seats.

"As you can see from all these pictures, we have quite a large family," I said, indicating the wall behind me, which was filled with framed photos. "These are the fifty-four wonderful children who make up our Nathaniel family. We have four sets of twins here. Laura and Loredana were brought to us after their mother and father divorced. This is their younger sister, Ionela," I said pointing to another picture. "She was only four years old when their mother left them. Imagine the fear, pain, and trauma she experienced when she realized her mother was leaving the family permanently. Behind every one of these beautiful, smiling faces is a tragic story.

"Here is another set of twins," I continued as I pointed out a dark complexioned boy and his sister. The dark eyes of Leon and Ramona gazed out of the photos at us. I explained that their mother placed them in a baby orphanage after their father abandoned the family. Later their Christian grandparents retrieved them and cared for them as long as they were able. After Leon and Ramona turned four, their grandparents brought them to our orphanage.

"From this family," I said as I pointed out four other photos, "we have two sets of twins. Ionuţ and Nicu are ten, and Cristi and Cristina are nine. Following a lengthy illness, their mother died of cancer, leaving eight children behind. Their father just couldn't make a living and also care for his children. He was forced to make a hard decision and chose to place his four youngest children under our care."

"Excuse me," said the leader, "but are these children ever adopted out? I mean, they are all beautiful children, and it appears to me there would be families who would want to adopt them. Is this not possible?" he asked.

"First of all," I began, "our charter makes no provision for adoption. So, by Romanian law, these children are not open for adoption. Second, most of our children have one living parent. The law requires the parent to visit the child at least once every six months. If they fail to do so, the court will reclassify the child as abandoned. The child then becomes eligible for adoption, but only if the child so desires."

"Do the children not want to be adopted?" asked a visitor.

"These children for the most part love it here, and the thought of adoption is frightening to them," I answered. "For most of them, this is the best home they have ever known.

"See this girl? Her name is Mihaela," I said as I pointed out the photo of a sandy-haired girl with a pleasant smile. "Her father had severe emotional problems and drank heavily. Four of their ten children are now part of our Nathaniel family.

"Mihaela had been here about four years when a friend invited her along for a home visit. I picked them up on the afternoon of the third day. As we traveled back to the orphanage, I asked, 'How did you girls enjoy your visit?' There was a slight pause, then Mihaela spoke up. 'It was all right,' she said, 'and we had a good time, but we were away too long.' Moments later she gave a deep sigh as we turned into the orphanage drive and said, 'It's so good to be *home!*' That is how most of our children feel," I concluded.

"Now I'd like to tell you how the Nathaniel Orphanage began." I took a deep breath. "In 1983 a young lady believer named Silvia, who grew up in Iaşi, Romania, was able to escape communist Romania and go to America. She had been under the surveillance of Ceauşescu's infamous security forces because she helped smuggle Bibles into Russia and taught children Christian values. She spent some time in a communist prison, where she thought she was going to die.

"When Silvia went to America she was invited to stay with the David Troyer family in Ohio. Two years earlier God had prompted Brother David to find some way to assist suffering Christians in Romania by shipping food parcels to augment their meager incomes. David began seeking the Lord, and a shipping and delivery network was formed whereby staples purchased in America could be safely shipped to needy Christian families in Romania. Christians here in Suceava were hired to oversee the distribution of those parcels. This was the beginning of what has become Christian Aid Ministries.

"Soon after Silvia arrived in America, David arranged for her to give presentations of her experiences in schools and to church groups. Many of these groups were Amish and Mennonite people who believed in making Christianity very practical. After hearing about the hardships experienced by Romanian Christian families under communism, these folks wanted to know how they could help. Silvia answered that if struggling Christian families in communist Romania could just receive a regular, supplementary food package it would make their lives so much easier and would prove to be a tremendous blessing to their children. She explained how much it would mean for these suffering families just to realize Christian brothers in America knew and cared about them.

"These American Christians responded by sharing the blessings God had given them," I explained, "and Christian Aid Ministries provided a safe and efficient way for them to give."

The Nathaniel Orphanage Family—1996

The four Biţica children, Marian, Elena, Stefania, and Vasilica (L to R above), were brought to the orphanage after police arrested their father. These traumatized children, who had watched helplessly as their father murdered their mother, found comfort and security with their new family.

Bill Mullet and the Romanian director, Ionica Bădiliţă, bid an emotional farewell at the train station.

Tina, Mama Ruth, and Oana share a special
moment at the little gray house.

The boys at Nathaniel Orphanage learn early the importance
of worshiping God in reverence and sincerity.

Manu, Gigi, and Costica (L to R) help snap string beans
from the orphanage garden.

Pavel enjoys his bottle of milk to the fullest. He, along with many of the other children, would hang around down at the farm, hoping to beg milk from the workers at the dairy processing lab. The workers were usually generous, and the children savored the treat, sometimes competing to see how long they could make their one-liter bottles last.

Marius and Iosif tenderly greet
the newlyhatched arrival.

Mariana smiles with the satisfaction
of having won the confidence of her
little feathered friend.

Pavel, Andi, Daniela, and Marius transfer two-week-
old chicks to a new and wider world.

FAMILY
ALBUM

Ovidiu Bădarau

Liviu Cherariu

David Baciu

Elena Bițica

Marian Bițica

Ștefania Bițica

Vasilica Bițica

Beni Bleoja

Monica Bleoja

Ionela Calancea

Laura Calancea

Loredana Calancea

Gigi Cimpoi

Adi Ciocan

Daniela Ciocan

Manu Ciocan

Larisa Cornea

Marius Cornea

Marinel Cozmiuc   Pavel Cruţ   Costel Cucuveica   Roxana Dicilov

Ioana Diculov   Davucu Dobrea   Lavinia Dobrea   Gabi Filan

Daniel Gheorgheş   Iosif Gheorgheş   Mariana Gheorgheş   Mihaela Gheorgheş

Andi Ifrose   Silviu Ifrose   Tina Ivaniou   Leon Ivanof

Ramona Ivanof   Nicoleta Mihalescu   Rodica Mihalescu   Beti Mocanu

Florentina Muntele

Ica Nicolaescu

Cristi Paduraru

Cristina Paduraru

Ionuț Paduraru

Nicu Paduraru

Bogdan Parnica

Gheorghe Parnica

Neli Parnica

Maria Parnica

Marta Parnica

Emanuela Petrescu

Cip Rǎducanu

Ioan Rǎducanu

Costicǎ Sandu

Iliuțǎ Sandu

Ștefi Sandu

Danuț Savin

Oana Savin

Florica Turcan

"How long did this go on?" someone asked.

"Food parcels are still being shipped to over two thousand needy Romanian families each month," I answered.

"During the eighties," I continued, "the communists held such tight control over visitors that it was nearly impossible for Americans to visit Romania. Then, in autumn of 1989, the revolution resulted in the execution of the dictator, Ceauşescu, and everything changed. David Troyer, Paul Weaver, and several other interested brethren made a trip to Romania in January of 1990. For the first time they could freely travel about Romania without being followed. This allowed them to visit places which would have been completely off limits only several months before. They visited state orphanages, and what they saw broke their hearts. They witnessed children suffering from being tied to their beds. Some desperately needed to be changed, and the stench was horrible. They saw children who were obviously afraid of the adult workers due to the abuse they had received. Watching them at mealtimes was like watching animals being fed. What they saw was so void of human compassion that they wept. They promised God that if He would open the doors, they would do something to ease the

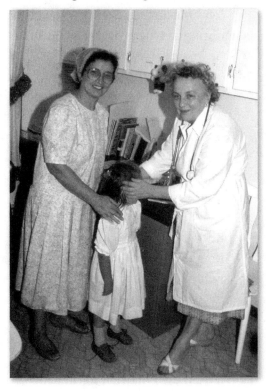

Faithful Nurse Viorica with
Florentina and the doctor

suffering of Romanian orphans. They made this promise in January of 1990, and in January of 1992 the first children entered this very room."

The visitors were leaning forward in their seats, and their intent expressions encouraged me to continue.

"I want to tell you one more story, then we'll get on with the tour." I stood and pointed to the picture of a round-faced little girl with large, dark eyes that peered back at us from under a head full of unruly hair. "This is Beti," I said. "She was placed in a baby orphanage as an infant and had almost no contact with her mother during the first three years of her life. By law, children may only remain in such institutions until they turn three, so her mother came forward to claim her. After a short time her mother disappeared, leaving Beti, not yet four years old, to fend for herself. Beti developed such a strong survival mentality during her time on the streets that the other children here have nicknamed her Beti Bulldozer.

"But this is getting ahead of my story," I continued. "One day, while roaming the streets of the village, Beti dashed out in front of an oncoming car and was hit. She fell onto the pavement, screaming with pain. The driver jumped out and ran to her. Seeing that she was injured, he picked her up, placed her in his car, and rushed her to a nearby hospital, where they determined that Beti had a broken collarbone.

"The nurses asked her family name, but the only name she knew was Beti. Next they asked her mother's name, but Beti had no idea. For the next two weeks the authorities tried to discover Beti's relatives through newspaper notices and radio broadcasts. She was finally identified by her grandparents, but her mother's whereabouts remained a mystery.

"The man who had hit her with his car had only one child, a seventeen-year-old son. He and his wife had not been able to have more children, so they decided to take Beti into their home, hoping to eventually adopt her. But everything seemed foreign to Beti, and she became frustrated at having to stay cooped up and not being allowed to roam the neighborhood freely as she was used to. One day in her anger she took a firm grip on the draperies of her new home and with a mighty wrench ripped those expensive curtains completely off the wall. On another occasion Beti became angry at mealtime. She vented her frustration by grabbing the tablecloth—with all the plates, glasses, silverware, and food on it—and jerking it off the table.

"About then, these would-be parents decided they were a bit too old to raise a child like Beti. And this is how Beti came to our orphanage. She is really an amazing little person in spite of her bulldozer disposition, and one cannot help but like her. The last chapter of her life is yet to be written, and we are watching to see what effects love will produce in her life.

"The couple who tried to adopt Beti have never forgotten her, and one day they drove three hours to come visit her. They had planned to take Beti back to their home for a week of vacation. They had looked forward to this for quite some time, and wanted to surprise Beti. But when they presented their plan, she flatly refused, saying, 'No. If I go away with you, I might never get to come back here again.'

"Our children entertain many fears," I explained, "but the fear of losing the love and security of the only real home they have ever known is one of their greatest."

I stood up, motioning to my attentive audience. "Follow me, and I'll show you around. Here's Sora Viorica's nurse's station, where she keeps the records for all the children. Besides the normal medical and school records, the Child Protection Agency requires five pages of hand-written annual reports on each child in our care. That's nearly three hundred hand-written papers to be submitted every year. Our Romanian workers joke that the dead in Romania are buried in dirt, but the living are buried in paper. I am finding this too true to be funny.

"Sora Viorica's main responsibility is to watch over the healthcare of the children. However, she also comes at any time, night or day, to see any worker who becomes ill. When anyone cuts a finger or burns himself down at the farm, this is where he comes for help. Neighbors from the area also come when they have medical problems, and she takes care of their needs whenever possible."

"Do the people pay her for the medicines?" asked a young lady in the tour group.

"No. Our medicines are donated, and we cannot sell donated goods," I answered.

"Come over this way, and everyone step up close. These photos show our orphanage activities. This group of eight children is working in our large garden. Here's another shot of girls pitting cherries. As you can see from the stains on their faces, not all the cherries went into the freezer. The children love to do things together. They have grown up this way and seem to find a sense of security in being together."

"What's this?" asked a young man as he leaned close to the bulletin board and pointed at a photo.

"That was last summer when we took a canoe trip down the Suceava River."

"You have canoes here?" asked the young man with obvious interest.

"We sure do," I confirmed. "Four of them. It's really fun, and I love to go with them. I even took my wife on a short trip one afternoon, though she doesn't swim. Many of the things we do with the children are to build bridges of communication and to create good memories," I explained. "We want to give them as nearly a normal, happy childhood as possible.

"Follow me into the dining room, and you can see where our

big family is served its meals. Can you imagine how much noise they generate when they are all eating and talking together? I have counted, and I estimate that at any given time during a meal at least thirty people are talking at once."

"Could you explain that wall chart?" asked a young lady from the group.

"The first column lists all the names of the children," I responded. "The rest of the columns represent the weeks of the year. The different colored stars tell at a glance the child's qualifications for that particular week."

"What do you mean by qualifications?" asked the leader.

"On each shift the daycare worker scores the behavior of each child under his or her care. At the end of the week these scores are averaged and a final score is given. A red star denotes excellent behavior and gives the child the right to go home with one of the workers for the weekend or to spend the night with a friend.

"And the gold?" asked an elderly woman.

"Gold stars tell you that this child had no serious infractions for the entire week. This earns privileges to play in the gym, play football, rollerblade, or to go away for the day with one of the workers. And the blue stars mean the child had several serious infractions, which means there will be a loss of privileges."

"In other words," commented the group leader, "it pays to be good."

"That's exactly what we are trying to teach these children," I agreed. "We want them to become responsible for their own actions."

"And is it working?" asked another member of the tour group.

"Look at this one," I said. "Daniela came from a godly home, but her mother died of cancer, and her father couldn't care for her. Last week she cried because she got a gold star instead of a red one. See," I pointed, "Daniela has eleven red stars in a row!

She really cares about being obedient, and it hurt her to be given a negative qualification. I wish we had more children like her," I finished wistfully, leading the group on.

"This is the kitchen. Allow me to introduce you to Roza, our head cook. Roza and I have been fighting since the day I arrived."

"Really?" said the leader.

"Well," I explained, "I have been fighting to keep from gaining too much weight, but Roza has been fixing temptingly good foods trying to make me gain weight. As you can see," I said, tapping my ample midriff, "Roza is winning." The group chuckled, and Roza gave me a perplexed look, since I had been speaking in English. I quickly switched to Romanian and explained, "I was just telling this group what a wonderful cook you are." Roza smiled at the compliment and went back to stirring the borscht she was preparing for supper.

We left the orphanage and followed the walks to the bakery. I showed the group our huge walk-in oven, the mixers, and the tables. I explained that the bakery was designed to bake bread and cookies for the orphanage and its workers.

"Do you have a store?" asked the leader.

"Not yet, but we do plan on building a store where our dairy products and baked goods can be sold," I explained. "But now back to the bakery. Our main reason for the bakery is to provide a safe place where our older girls can learn a marketable skill in a godly atmosphere. We choose our bakery employees for their Christian character as well as their baking skills."

"And must the workers have a certificate of baking?" asked the leader.

"Certainly," I responded. "And in addition to holding certificates showing extensive studies in baking, they must also have health certificates. Once we begin selling our baked goods we can only produce products that have been approved by the state inspectors.

If we want to bake a cookie using a new recipe, we must first go through the red tape of getting that recipe approved by the state."

"Really?" said one of the ladies from the group, "I didn't expect Romania to be so—controlling."

"Romania has only been out from under communist rule for nine years, so the mentality of the government officials is still rather controlling," I explained as I led them through the door and toward the school building.

We entered the gym, where fourth grade was having physical education. Together we watched as their teacher divided the children into two groups. She skillfully organized them into competing teams and demonstrated maneuvers using a basketball to develop coordination, accuracy, and stamina.

"Are these children all from this orphanage?" asked the tour leader.

"No," I responded. "There are four children who attend our school but are not a part of our orphanage. Three are our workers' children, and one is from a neighboring family."

"I think it is good for your children to interact with children from normal families," said one young lady.

"Yes," I agreed, "we feel it's good for them to form friendships outside the orphanage. Sometimes they get to spend a night in a classmate's home."

Just then the teacher dismissed the children for break. Costel took off running after Marian, and Ionela chased after Costel. "Copii (children)!" I shouted above the noise of the children at play. "Come. I want you to meet our visitors. They have traveled here from far-off Norway."

Davucu came up and, like a little man, soberly shook hands with several of the tour group. Costel strode up and said, "Hi." Ionela also came over and welcomed them. Those in the tour group who spoke English were delighted to discover that they could converse directly with the children. For the next five minutes they enjoyed a lively discussion. Many asked questions about living in the orphanage, how they liked school, and what they wanted to become when they grew up.

The children were soon called back to their classrooms and lessons. I led the tour group to visit the third grade, where we observed the teacher and students in action.

"Notice Mihaela," I whispered. "She's that cute little girl standing on the bench so she can reach the blackboard. Watch how she works that five-step algebra problem." Sure enough, after several false starts and one erasure, Mihaela correctly worked the problem, received a word of praise from her teacher, and flashed me a bright smile as she took her seat.

"Algebra," I explained as we walked on down the hallway, "actually begins in the second grade and becomes the principle form of math throughout the rest of their schooling. All their math is worked horizontally instead of in vertical columns as I was taught. I find it embarrassing, but I can hardly help the fourth-grade students with their math lessons," I confessed.

I knocked on a door marked "Sewing."

"May we come in?" I asked.

"Sure," came a pleasant voice. We all crowded into a small room where Veronica sat at a sewing machine. She smiled as she rose to greet our guests. After introductions, I explained that Veronica was our full-time seamstress.

"Sora Veronica, what are you working on today?" I asked. She held up a partially finished dress and explained that it was a birthday dress for Florica.

"Oh, Florica will love it," I said, admiring its bright yellow color. "You see," I went on, "every child gets a new outfit for his birthday. The girls get new dresses of their choice, and the boys receive trousers and dress shirts. Of course they receive other clothing throughout the year, but this is special, because it's for their birthdays."

I thanked Veronica and led our group out of doors as I continued talking. "Florica is from a Gypsy family, and her mother died while she was quite young. Her father brought her here to become a part of our Nathaniel family because he didn't feel he could raise her alone. Sometimes I wonder if we can raise her." I chuckled as I shook my head. "She reminds me of a young, untamed horse galloping through life. But you ought to hear her sing! She has amazing natural ability. Incidentally, she and I share the same birthday, and that means a lot to her."

As we walked toward the church, we passed our little gray house. I explained that this was where I lived with my wife and three children. "This little house was originally used as a chicken house, but the chickens didn't do well. I believe it was because our location here is some six hundred miles farther north than where we lived in America. In the fall, without controlled lighting, the decrease in daylight hours causes the chickens to quit laying eggs. Since the chickens that lived in this house didn't do well, they were all butchered, and the house was remodeled. Now I live here, and believe me, I'm trying to be sure I do well," I laughed. "I have no desire to experience the same fate!"

We arrived at the Nathaniel Church and entered. They looked at the high cathedral ceiling finished in natural native pine and the matching pulpit and wainscoting. There was a holy hush among our visitors as they took it all in. The leader spoke for a moment with his group, and one of the young ladies led a Christian hymn in their native Norwegian. It was truly beautiful!

As the echoes of their song died away, I rose and faced them. I told them of the Biţica children and the tragic loss of their mother. I explained how she was murdered by their father before their very eyes and how their father was taken away by the police. I explained how their little world came crashing hopelessly down around them, all in one day. Then I said, "But the greatest miracle of God's grace is to see how these children have so completely forgiven their father. Hardly a Wednesday evening goes by without one of the four raising their little hands to say, 'Please pray for our father, that he will repent.' And these children really pray for their father."

"Where is their father?" asked the group leader.

"I wish I knew," I answered. "I have tried to trace him through the prison system, but we have not been able to shake one bit of information out of the prison authorities. I want Mr. Biţica to know that his children are well taken care of, that they love him, that they have forgiven him, and that they continue to pray for his salvation." Several in the group wiped tears from their eyes as I finished the story.

Soon we were back outside, headed for the farm.

"We raise as many fresh vegetables as we can," I explained as we passed the garden. "We raise enough peas for the freezer and several hundred heads of cabbage. We also raise snap beans for the season and produce tomatoes, onions, carrots, cauliflower, and broccoli. We believe it is important for our children to learn how to raise a good garden."

"I see you have an orchard," observed one young man.

"That we do, and we have been getting red and yellow delicious apples from these trees," I explained.

By then we'd arrived at the farm.

"As you can see, we have Holstein cows," I explained. "The older cows you are looking at were donated to CAM in 1993 as young heifers and were flown from Philadelphia, Pennsylvania, to Bucureşti, Romania. From there they were trucked here to Suceava."

"They really came from America on an airplane?" interjected the group leader.

"Yes," I said, smiling at the look of surprise on his face. "Ninety-six bred heifers were flown here to give us the genetics we felt were needed to begin a herd of heavy-producing milk cows. At that time very few milk cows with good bloodlines were available in Romania."

From here I took them into the laboratory where the milk was processed and bottled for distribution. I explained that we donated milk to eighteen orphanages and several church groups. "In many cases children would have to go without milk if we were not here to supply it for them."

"But how can you afford to just give it away? It must be expensive to produce the milk," said the leader.

"Sponsors in America and Canada donate money every month so we can make milk available to those in need." I explained that certain orphanage boys were chosen daily to help our hired workers feed and milk the cows, learning firsthand about dairying. The girls helped produce ice cream.

As we left the milk processing area and headed up the cement drive toward the orphanage, I fielded more questions.

"What are you going to do when these children turn eighteen? Will they be forced out of the orphanage?"

"Allow me to turn that question around," I said. "Would you turn your children out of your homes when they turn eighteen?"

"Well, no," they answered.

"Neither do we want to turn these children out when they reach eighteen. We want to provide for them as we would our very own. The government forces children out of state-funded orphanages at age eighteen. Many become homeless and turn to stealing or prostitution to sustain themselves. We do not receive funds from the government, so we are free to provide for our children until they are able to support themselves."

"Will they go on to college?" asked a young man.

"We want these children to become productive Romanian citizens. If the children feel led to a profession needing a college education, then that will certainly be open to them," I explained.

By now we had circled back to their van.

"It has been such a blessing to see what you are doing for these children," the spokesman said. "God bless you in this work, and we hope you stay here a long time with these children."

"God be with you as you go," I said. "And remember to pray for us, because this isn't our work. It's the Lord's."

CHAPTER 13

THE CONTEST

"Someone is here to see you," announced Manu as he passed my office early in the afternoon. "I think it's Pavel's older brother."

I met the young man in the living room and welcomed him.

"I am Pavel's brother," he announced, "and I'd like to see Pavel, if I may," he added pleasantly.

Pavel's mother had died in a tragic car accident when he was only four years old. His father had eleven children to care for and soon realized he couldn't manage. He struggled with the idea of giving up any of his children, but finally saw that he had no choice and brought Pavel to the Nathaniel Christian Orphanage.

Pavel had a very sensitive nature, was easy to teach, and wanted to do his best in any given task. Later his father remarried, but soon separated, partly due to his heavy drinking. We feared for Pavel's well-being whenever he was left with his family for any length of time. He was fearful and anxious for several days following each visit. While I was glad his family still wanted to be involved with him, I couldn't help feeling concerned about the effects of this visit.

I sent one of the boys upstairs to bring Pavel to meet his brother and left them visiting in the living room while I returned to catch up on my office work. Soon Pavel's brother showed up at my office door. "Would you give me permission to take Pavel home for a visit?" he asked.

"You know," I said cautiously, "Ionică is gone, and I cannot let Pavel go until we've had an opportunity to discuss this with him."

"Just for one week?" he begged.

"No," I repeated, my mind now firmly made up. "We must clear this with Ionică."

"Okay. When will he be back?" he asked.

"He plans to return on Tuesday," I replied.

Two weeks passed before Pavel's brother returned. Ionică explained how unsettled Pavel had become following his last visit home, but granted permission, with the stipulation that any activity that would upset Pavel's sensitive nature had to be avoided. All were in agreement, and the papers were signed allowing Pavel to spend a week in his home and to be brought back to the orphanage by July 7.

A gnawing worry set in when July 7 came and went with no sign of Pavel. Another week passed.

"This isn't right," Ionică said. "We must go find Pavel. Who knows what might become of him if we allow this to continue? We have a legal responsibility for him."

"We're not sure we can really trust his family," added Vali. "This is why the agreement was for one week only."

After several more days of waiting and considerable discussion about what we should do, Vali and Nurse Viorica left for the village of Vicov to see if they could locate Pavel. They found his house, but no one was home, and they were appalled at its obvious disarray and neglect. Vali asked the neighbors if Pavel had been there.

"Yes, Pavel was here for a few days, but then was taken to a monastery," a helpful neighbor lady told Vali.

This story sounded pretty far-fetched to Vali. "Oh, come on," he said disbelievingly. "What would be the point in placing a nine-year-old boy in a monastery?"

"The stepmother lives in a nearby village. She may know more about it," offered the neighbor. "Perhaps you should talk with her."

Pavel's ten-year-old brother arrived as they were discussing what should be done. He said he knew where his stepmother lived and would be willing to show them the way.

The stepmother confirmed that Pavel had indeed been taken to a monastery. She confided that she had overheard Pavel's father and brothers planning this before asking permission for the visit.

"You see," she explained, "Pavel has an older brother who is studying to become an Orthodox priest, and his superiors will not allow him to advance further if any members of his immediate family are under the direct influence of evangelical Christian teaching. Please go get him and take him back to the Nathaniel Orphanage," she begged. "I know that's the best place for him."

"How do we find this monastery?" Vali asked.

Pavel's stepmother gladly gave directions, and they were soon on their way.

The road was rough and winding, and it took them half an hour to arrive at the foot of the mountain upon which the monastery was located. Vali turned off the main road and onto the Jeep track that wound its way up over the rough terrain. It was rugged, but the scenery was absolutely beautiful.

As they traveled farther up the mountain, the road became more and more difficult. Vali finally realized it was foolhardy to drive on, so, after parking by the side of the trail and securely locking the car, they started out on foot. The mountain became quite steep and the going was rough.

After forty-five minutes they crested the mountain and came

to a place where the land became more level and open. As they descended the far side of the mountain, they entered a cultivated area of fields and pastures belonging to the monastery. Here and there, monks were busy raking and forking hay onto drying racks. Vali stopped beside one of the younger monks and engaged him in conversation. In spite of his austere black robe, he seemed friendly enough, but he said he hadn't seen a boy who fit Pavel's description.

Later they stopped and talked with another monk, who was also working in the fields.

"Oh, yes," he said, "Pavel Cruț has been here almost a week visiting his brother who is studying to become a priest. Just go on up to the main building and talk with the priest there. He'll be glad to help you," he offered.

Finally they reached the monastery itself. It was a forbidding stone edifice surrounded by several houses and a stone wall. They entered at a large wrought iron gate and walked up the gravel path to the monastery. The recently scythed hay inside the wall perfumed the air with a fresh, sweet aroma. A young man intercepted them and asked pleasantly if he could be of help. He was dressed in a flowing, brown robe, and his face was partially masked by a youngish-looking, soft, brown beard. His hair was long and tied at the nape of his neck.

"Yes," said Vali. "We're from the Nathaniel Christian Orphanage, and we're looking for a nine-year-old boy named Pavel Cruț. We were told he is here, and we would like to speak with him."

"There's no one here by that name," responded the young man.

Viorica spoke up, "I am a registered nurse. I work for the orphanage, and I take care of all the children's records. Pavel was taken by his brother to visit his father nearly three weeks ago, with permission to stay one week only. He still hasn't returned," she explained. "If the Child Protection Agency inspects us now, we could be in trouble. So we have come to take him back to the orphanage. Please tell us where he is."

"I've already told you," persisted the young man, "there's no one here by that name."

"We have very direct information that he is here, and we don't intend to leave until he is in our care," Vali stated firmly.

"Please sit down," the young man said as he offered chairs to Viorica and Vali. "I don't know how I can help you. There's no one here by that name."

"Perhaps he's not here now," said Vali, "but you know where he is."

Following a lengthy discussion, the young man excused himself and said, "Wait here; let me ask my superior. Perhaps he knows something."

The student priest soon returned with his superior. Following a round of polite greetings, the superior asked, "What seems to be the problem here?" Vali explained the situation once more, and the older priest said, "Let me check this out. I'll be right back." The student priest continued talking with them, then finally revealed his identity. He was, in fact, Pavel's older brother.

As they waited, the sound of a motor shattered the stillness of the mountain air. Vali turned toward the sound and saw three men on a tractor preparing to leave the monastery.

Finally the elderly priest returned. "I have good news for you," he announced. "I was able to find the boy you are looking for. I will give you directions to the house where he can be found. The family's name is Cozac, and he's living with them." Pavel's brother left and came back shortly with a pen and paper. The elderly priest wrote down directions to the Cozac home. Vali thanked them for their help, took the offered directions, and shook hands as he bade them goodbye.

After a brisk, thirty-minute walk back to the car, they began gingerly winding their way down the mountain track. As they approached an intersection in the mountain road, an ancient green Aro jeep entered the road just ahead of them. Vali got a good look at the driver and his two passengers. He was surprised to recognize the same three men he had seen leaving the monastery on the tractor. The road was narrow and it was impossible to pass, so Vali followed them. Viorica read aloud from the written directions. When they came to the turnoff where they should bear left toward the Cozacs' village, the Aro turned left ahead of them.

As they got to the village, the Aro turned left again and led them directly to the Cozac home. Vali and the men from the monastery arrived just moments apart. He and Viorica scrambled out of the car and joined the men as they moved toward the house. Viorica waited outside while Vali entered with them. There, in the corner of the room, he found Pavel, noticeably thinner, dirty, and in need of fresh clothing.

"Pavel," said Vali, placing his arm around his shoulders, "I've come to take you back to the orphanage." Pavel stood up. His face was grim, and he seemed relieved to see Vali. The other men were watching, and there was tension in the air.

"Are you ready?" Vali asked. Pavel nodded, and Vali said, "Let's go." They walked past the men through the door to where Viorica was waiting for them. As they climbed into the car, Viorica asked, "Pavel, where are your clothes?"

"Oh, I forgot them," he said. "They're inside."

"You can't leave them here," said Viorica. "Go get them." Pavel hopped out of the car and hurried back into the house. Five minutes passed. Vali looked at his watch, then at Viorica, eyebrows raised. Ten minutes passed, and still no Pavel. Exasperated, Vali got out and strode toward the door. Entering the small house, he saw one of the older men from the monastery bent over, his face only inches from Pavel's, speaking gruffly and looking angry. Pavel was crying.

Vali took Pavel by the hand and said, "Pavel, come with me." The man from the monastery fixed his gaze on Pavel's face. Pavel hesitated for a moment.

"Come, Pavel," said Vali, deciding to leave the clothing behind. He tugged on Pavel's arm. Slowly, Pavel followed Vali to the door. On the way to the car, Vali wondered just what it was the older man had been saying that had made Pavel reluctant to return to the orphanage. As they drove away, Pavel was crying. He was unusually quiet upon arriving at the orphanage and spent much time in his room. He seemed very unhappy.

We soon discovered that his brother and the other priests had given Pavel intense religious instruction while he was with them. Pavel's sensitive nature and his desire to do what was right had caused him to become deeply confused.

That evening I went up to Pavel's bedroom and tried to help him. I explained that there's nothing in the Bible that says we are to make the sign of the cross. Neither is there anything in the Bible that would indicate that we should pray to Mary or to the holy saints, as he had been instructed.

At seven o'clock the next morning a priest arrived at the orphanage. Vali refused to allow the priest to speak with Pavel, and the priest left, saying he would be back later.

Pavel seemed disturbed and confused about spiritual matters. At the end of each mealtime prayer he insisted on making the sign of the cross. He talked to the other boys about life in the monastery, the burning of candles, praying to the saints, and the rhythmic beating of the prayer board. He spoke affectionately of dusting the icons and of being in the monastery with his older brother. At the same time he appeared very mixed up emotionally. He was sad, downcast, and melancholy. Ionică took Pavel into his own home for the first several nights to discuss biblical truths and to help him reestablish a sense of well-being and contentment. It was devastating to Ionică to realize that five years of training and teaching had seemingly all melted away after less than two weeks at the monastery.

On Wednesday I returned from town with several orphanage children, turned into the driveway of the orphanage, and parked. As I stepped out of the car, an old, green Aro pulled up and parked just outside the open orphanage gate. A monk in long black robes stepped out and walked toward me. He had a young boy with him. It was Pavel's ten-year-old brother. I shook hands cordially and welcomed them.

He said he would like to talk with Pavel for a few minutes in private. I explained that he was welcome to speak with Pavel, but only in my presence. Pavel came into my office, and as they talked I sat behind my desk working. Although I appeared to be preoccupied with my work, I was listening intently to their conversation. The monk began telling Pavel that he would return within several days to take him back to the monastery.

"Just one moment, sir," I interrupted. "Pavel has been placed here by the Child Protection Agency. He is legally under our care, and we are responsible to the Romanian government for him."

"Oh, I understand," said the monk with a show of respect. However, he then turned to Pavel and continued, "As I was saying, I'll be back in several days to pick you up and take you to the monastery."

At this point I opened a file drawer and produced papers showing that we were legally responsible for Pavel. "You may continue talking with Pavel if you like, but we will have no more talk whatsoever about taking him away."

The monk ignored me and continued telling Pavel that he would definitely return to pick him up. Then, turning to me, he said, "When I do come back, I will also have papers, and I *will* take Pavel with me!"

"I won't tolerate this kind of talk in my office. If you plan on continuing to talk this way, you will have to leave."

"Okay, okay," said the black-robed monk. "I understand."

His next question was, "May Pavel and his brother play together?" I feared further treachery, and explained that it was almost suppertime, and that I would not give permission for them to play together. But I thought it might be good for our records to have photographic proof that this monk had been to our orphanage trying to persuade Pavel to return to the monastery, so I whipped out my camera and asked the monk, Pavel, and his brother to stand together for a photo so Pavel could place it in his album. The three stood close together. But the few seconds it took for my camera to load its flash gave the monk enough time to reconsider being photographed in my office with Pavel. Before I could focus my camera, the monk stepped out of view, stating that I should take the photo with just Pavel and his brother. I took my photo without the object I so desired, and the monk soon left, taking Pavel's brother with him.

Several weeks passed, and we had no more visits from the monastery. Pavel began to find his place among his friends in the orphanage again. But the experience convinced me that a contest was on, and the prize was the souls of these precious children.

CHAPTER 14

INSPECTED

Ionică had taken the nurse and seven of the girls to the dentist and wouldn't return for several hours. During his absence a lady showed up unexpectedly. She announced that she was from the President's Department in Bucureşti and was here to make an inspection. She approached one of our workers and demanded, "Where is your director? I want to speak with him."

Our bewildered worker stammered, "I—I really don't know where he is."

The visitor paced, obviously agitated, then went over to the school building. She looked into several of the classrooms, then returned to the kitchen and tersely demanded, "Where is your American director?" Another worker shrugged and replied, "I'm not sure where he is either."

I don't know why the worker didn't offer to look for me. She just kept on with her kitchen duties as though nothing else were important. All this time I was a mere fifty yards away in the new bakery installing a heating system.

Our visitor became angry and began ranting. Children gathered as they usually do when there is a disturbance. The official raised her voice in anger and accusingly announced, "You people are holding these children prisoners! Furthermore," she shouted angrily as she waved her arms about, "you are indoctrinating them with your religion of evangelical Christianity. The religion of Romania is Orthodox, and these children are Romanians! They must be taught Orthodox Church doctrines! Why aren't you teaching them the practices of the Orthodox Church?" Without waiting for an answer, she continued her tirade. "I have just come from your school building, and you're not even supposed to have a school here! You have no authorization for a school! I am going straight to the police to have this place shut down at once!"

Our poor kitchen worker stood there, dumbfounded. Then, looking past the visitor, she saw stark fear in the eyes of the girls who had gathered in the hallway. If this woman closed down their home, where would they go? What would happen to them?

Seven-year-old Florentina held her hand over her mouth, aghast at what she had just heard. Her classmate Tina went dashing down the hall to her classroom. "Teacher! Teacher!" she shouted. "Did you hear what that woman said? She said she's going . . ."

"What woman?" interrupted the teacher.

"The lady who came into our classroom while you were teaching our math lesson," replied Tina. "She said we're not supposed to have a school here. And she said you are teaching us the wrong religion. And she said she was going to go get the police and make the Americans go away. And they are going to close down our orphanage. Teacher, where will we sleep? I don't like that woman. She's angry, and she talked very loud to our cook!"

"Yes, and without respect too," came the sober observation from Florentina, who had followed Tina.

"And she was real red in her face," added Mihaela in a serious, sad voice.

"Where's the woman now?" asked the teacher.

"She got in her car and left," reported Larisa, who up until now had only watched and listened.

News of the woman's visit spread through the orphanage like wildfire. Children and workers alike talked of nothing else.

When Ionică returned from the dentist, he had barely climbed out of the van when he was bombarded by a large group of children all talking at once about the woman from the president's office. He looked perplexed as he tried to make heads or tails out of all that was being said. Finally he understood enough to make his way into the orphanage to speak directly with the kitchen workers. He was quiet as the sobering truth soaked in that there were people looking for ways to close down our orphanage—people who would readily sacrifice these children for political reasons.

Ionică asked, "Who was this woman? What was her name? Did anyone ask to see her credentials?" Somehow, no one had thought to ask our visitor those crucial questions. Ionică shook his head and said he would look into this incident. After reassuring the frightened children that he didn't think this woman could actually close down our orphanage, he led them in for supper, and the atmosphere stabilized. However, the incident troubled him deeply. He prayed about it, and a plan formed in his mind.

The next Tuesday a governmental meeting was scheduled in Suceava for nonprofit organizations that received no support from the Romanian government. Ionică planned to attend. Topics included laws regulating nonprofit organizations and advice on how we were to prepare and present records for government officials.

Following this lengthy meeting, Ionică was given permission to ask several questions. He began by telling the officials that he represented the Nathaniel Christian Orphanage, where fifty-four children lived together in one big family. He then told them of the visitor who had come unannounced from the president's office. He repeated the things she had said and the threats she had made. After he had their full attention, Ionică asked, "Who was this woman, and who sent her to come inspect our facilities? What was her mission?"

The moderator looked a bit ill at ease and responded evasively, but Ionică was not one to be put off so easily. He tried again.

"Gentlemen," he addressed the assembly, "I have worked for CAM for nearly six years. I am a Romanian, and I try to always respect Romanian law. If I have failed in some point, tell me. If there is something about our organization that needs to be corrected, inform us. Our desire is to do what is right and what is best for the children under our care. This woman's visit was very unsettling to our children, and I want to get to the bottom of this. Who was she? Was she really from the president's office? Would someone please answer me?"

Once again Ionică's questions were brushed aside. Their obvious discomfort made him suspect they knew more than they were telling.

Ionică thought he would try a different tactic. "How many of you have never seen our orphanage and farm?" he asked. A number acknowledged that they had never been there.

"I am giving you a personal invitation to come visit our orphanage and see for yourselves just how we operate. When will it suit you to come?" Ionică asked as he pressed his point.

There was a hum of discussion around the table, and it was decided that they would come after lunch. With that promise in hand, Ionică excused himself and left.

When Ionică arrived at the orphanage, he received a message from his wife in Cluj that his daughter Iulia was to undergo open heart surgery the next day. He would have to leave on the evening train.

Ionică gathered the workers and children and informed them of the impending visit. "Let's work until they arrive to get this place squeaky clean," he added.

And how they did work! The bathrooms were scrubbed,

although they were not particularly dirty. Carpets that had been vacuumed that morning were gone over again. One of the older girls washed the window in the front door, and a boy emptied trashcans. All hands were very busy for the next hour and a half. Soon one of the boys came rushing downstairs shouting, "They're here! Look at those cars!"

"Boys," said the tanti sharply, "get away from that window, and stop pulling back those curtains. Come here!" she commanded.

Ionică welcomed our honored guests personally. They had come in two chauffeured cars. One was the president of the Suceava Veterinarian Association, another was the vice prefect of Suceava County, and another was an adviser to the president. A woman who filled a similar post stepped out of the second car, followed by another man who was an unidentified cog in the governmental gears.

Ionică was on home turf. I could see that he enjoyed guiding this tour. He began in the big living room of the orphanage and led them past the photos of the children. He paused to explain several case histories and to answer their questions. Children stood shyly off to the side, watching. Then, of all things, Ionică paused to show them the ladies' restroom! Romania still had many public restrooms that were nothing more than small concrete cubicles with holes in the floor. I was a bit appalled that Ionică chose to show them our restroom, but the visitors seemed impressed with its cleanliness and the multiple sinks and toilets.

Next he took them through the dining room and into the kitchen, where they observed a huge supper being prepared for our large family of hungry children. They looked with interest at our walk-in refrigerator and the fresh fruits and vegetables in it. They meandered upstairs to the dormitories, where they nosed into several of the bedrooms and spoke personally with the children. I could tell they were impressed.

We went through the gym, and Ionică stopped briefly at our

Gospel literature distribution office. He boldly told them about the literature that was distributed from this office. He then led them through the classrooms. The visitors showed an even greater interest in this part of the tour. They had questions about the school and its authorization. They asked whether the teachers were Romanian or American, and whether the teaching was done in English or Romanian.

Ionică responded, "We use only certified Romanian teachers. We use the state curriculum, which is taught in Romanian. Yes, we do have authorization from the government to operate this school, grades one through four. We have applied to extend that authorization to grades five through eight." Ionică answered every question to their satisfaction.

All this while I stayed in the background, tagging along at the end of the group. After we visited the school, Ionică led us out onto the second-story landing before descending the stairs toward the farm. From the landing he pointed out the bakery, which was almost completed, and the garden where we raised many of our own vegetables. He pointed to the generator house, which housed a huge Caterpillar engine ready to take up temporary duty should the current from the power company fail.

"And do the older children help with the gardening?" asked one of the visitors.

"Yes, they do. We feel it is important for these children to learn to provide for themselves as much as possible," explained Ionică.

I saw the visitors' heads nodding in agreement, and I began to feel more positive about this visit.

As we stood on the landing looking over the neatly clipped lawn of lush green grass, it reminded me somewhat of a picture postcard. It was truly beautiful. One of the government officials must have thought so too, for he leaned close to me and asked in clipped British English, "The beautiful grass . . . is it American or Romanian?"

I thought frantically, *If I tell him this grass is from seed imported from America, it might sound as if I don't think Romanian grass is good enough for us.* So I said, "The seed is American, but the grass is Romanian." My response tickled the official, and I heard him chuckle as he repeated it to his fellow visitors in Romanian, which he no doubt thought I couldn't understand.

We showed them Stela and Steluţa in the horse barn. They wanted to know if any of the children rode the horses. Ionică explained that the children often rode the mare with proper supervision, but that the younger horse was still in training.

Alvin then joined us for a tour of the farm. He explained that our cows were donated by American farmers and were flown over on a special chartered flight. He spoke of our program to make free milk available to children in other orphanages and to provide a place where our boys could learn to work as they matured. The vet was especially interested in this portion of the tour, and he and Alvin talked about the cows while the others visited the overly friendly calves in their hutches. Alvin explained how we allow our livestock plenty of fresh air, even in the winter. He then showed them the milk processing plant and the ice cream machine.

"Oh yes!" exclaimed one of the men. "I eat this ice cream and like it very much!"

We left the farm and walked back up to the orphanage living room, where we took photos standing with the government officials and had them sign our orphanage guestbook. We stood in the parking lot and watched as the last car rolled out the gate. Ionică and I looked at each other and spontaneously said in unison, "*Slavă Dumnului!* (Praise the Lord!)"

Some months later two agents from the Suceava Health Department visited. By Romanian law a septic waste system has to empty into flowing water if it is within reasonable distance. Ours passed through a filter bed before emptying into a sizable creek several hundred yards away. Two ladies had come to take samples of this runoff water for testing. I had to smile to myself as I watched these fashionably-dressed career women traipsing through our dew-wet pasture to the creek far below our barn. But I soon forgot about our visitors as I went on with my work.

Our teacher had asked me to read her English text for the day into a recorder and sing the little song she was teaching the children. She was unfamiliar with the song and wanted the accent to be correct. She instructed me to speak slowly and distinctly into the recorder for the benefit of the children, who knew very little English.

I carefully closed the door to my office and began to read the text with agonizing slowness. I also clarified words that might give the students difficulty. Then I came to the song. I smiled to myself as I sang into the mike. "Old MacDonald had a farm, e-i, e-i-oooh." I sang with exaggerated slowness, breaking each syllable and over-emphasizing the pronunciation for clarity. I progressed to MacDonald's cow with its "moo, moo here," and its "moo, moo there, here a moo, there a moo, everywhere a moo, moo . . ."

I worked my way through the verses of Old MacDonald's dogs' "bow wows," his ducks' "quack quacks," and his hens' "cluck clucks." I finished recording the tape just minutes before the English class was to begin and delivered it to a very pleased teacher. I returned to my office with a feeling of accomplishment and looked about for the next most important project to tackle.

Vali stepped into my office just then and asked, "Johnny, what have you been doing?"

"I was preparing a tape for the third grade English class," I said a bit sheepishly, thinking how my recording must have sounded to him as he sat in the next office.

"You've created quite a sensation," he said, smiling.

"What do you mean?" I asked.

"Well," he explained, "do you remember the two ladies who came this morning from the Health Department?"

"Yes. Were they able to collect the water they needed?"

"They sure did. The last time they were here they threatened to close us down because they found too high a bacteria count in our runoff water. We tried to correct this problem with a chlorination station, and today they came for a re-test. If we fail this test, we will really be in trouble with the authorities."

"All right," I said, "but what does all this have to do with creating a sensation?"

"Those fancy ladies collected their two-liter bottle of water and returned to my office with legal papers for me to sign. They were just leaving when you began singing about cows saying "moo, moo." I glanced into the hallway, and you should have seen them!" he laughed. "They were leaning close to your office door, listening intently, absolutely perplexed! 'Who is in there?' they asked me. 'Our American director,' I informed them. Then you went into a series of 'bow wows.' The ladies looked at each other with raised eyebrows and just shook their heads," he chuckled.

I'm not sure whether it was the chlorine or the song, but after that we had very little trouble with the sewage inspectors.

The orphanage was at the edge of town on a piece of land where people from Iţcani had dumped their trash for many years. Garbage, tin cans, busted up concrete slabs, old plaster, and bedsprings had to be cleared away before the construction could begin. A wrought-iron fence had been built around the property, but old habits die slowly. So the inhabitants of Iţcani still loaded their refuse onto wagons or push carts and dumped it just beyond the corner of our fence on land belonging to the state farm. This was not only unsightly, but drew mice, flies, and other vermin. We complained to the authorities numerous times. Finally they sent a crew with a movie camera to catch the perpetrators on film. I supposed they intended to expose these people and air their "catch" on the local TV station.

These "experts" took up a position of surveillance in our orphanage dining room, facing the huge pile of fermenting rubbish. In all the hours they sat fingering their cameras, not one person showed up to dump trash. The day after they left, the dumping resumed, and the ugly heap grew larger and larger.

After all our experiences with inspectors, I thought I had met every kind of inspector that existed. Then one day a man walked in and announced that he was the fly inspector from the Suceava Health Department. I wondered just how he was going to inspect our flies. Was he really worried about their health? He told me that if he found an unacceptable number of flies in our facilities he would demand that we have all of our walls sprayed with a potent fly killer. He explained that this poison had an effective life span of six months. I wondered about the toxic effects on children.

Reminding myself that prevention is better than cure, I asked him to follow me and led him through the orphanage and over to the corner of the fence. "Take a look at that," I said to the inspector as I pointed to the garbage heap, which was abuzz with flies.

"That is a problem!" said the inspector emphatically. "And just whose property is it?" he asked as he whipped out a notepad and pen.

"That property belongs to the government," I answered. "It is the state farm's land."

"Oh," replied the inspector, slowly replacing his notepad without having written one word. "That *is* a problem!"

In the end he ordered that all the walls in the orphanage be treated with fly killer spray, but absolutely nothing was done about the growing pile of trash just outside our fence.

For a number of years all our petitions fell upon deaf ears. Then one day we were told that the American ambassador was coming to our area, and the local Romanian authorities were bringing him to visit the Nathaniel Christian Orphanage. The morning before the ambassador arrived, a government-ordered dump truck and loader removed the unsightly mess. The Iţcanians, distrusting the government's new interest in the area, found someplace else to dump their trash.

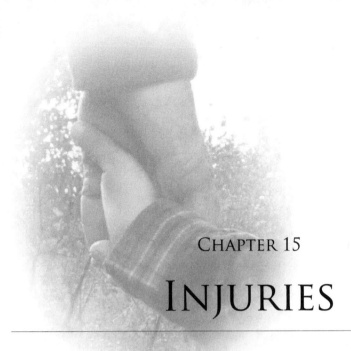

CHAPTER 15

INJURIES

Vasile brought me the good news that he had completed the chicken plucker. It was finished just in time, because our next batch of broilers was almost ready.

On Friday evening many willing hands helped me position the funnels, scalder, and plucker in their respective places in the clean, unused portion of the little animal barn. The boys had so many questions.

"Do you have to kill the chickens before you put them in the machine?" asked Marius.

"How will this take the feathers off the chickens?" asked Marian.

I explained that the disc at the bottom of the drum was powered by an electric motor and would spin, causing its rubber fingers to rub the feathers from the scalded chickens.

"But that won't work," commented Leon. "It will only take the feathers off the bottom side of the chickens."

"Well, if it works like it should," I said, "the chickens will tumble and turn every which way so all the feathers come in contact with those moving fingers. You'll see. If we scald the chickens for just the right amount of time, this machine will do a fine job of cleaning the chickens without tearing their skin.

That evening as I told the boys goodnight, they couldn't stop talking about the new chicken plucker and what fun we would have the next day.

After our usual Saturday morning pancake breakfast, we had our devotional time. Then several adult workers helped organize the butchering operation, and the boys carried the broilers from their pens. As soon as the first six were killed and scalded, the boys gathered closely to watch this new

The chicken plucker in action

machine in operation. Would it really work? Some were doubtful.

I started the machine, adjusted the water flow, and dropped in the first two broilers. I am sure no two chickens in Romania ever had more eyes riveted upon their de-featheration than did those two. Children clung to the framework of the machine. Others climbed the bracing of the barn wall, and a few even climbed into the rafters to get a bird's-eye view of the action. The spraying water, flying feathers, and flopping chickens thrilled the children. Others hollered to workers who happened by to come in and see. They laughed, pointed, and jabbered in Romanian much faster than my ability to understand. They got the biggest kick out of watching the chickens "dance" in the new machine as their feathers were shed. So many boys climbed up to see what was happening inside the plucker that I had to move boys before I could drop in more chickens. They needed repeated reminders to keep on working with the other aspects of butchering. Tables had been set up and quite a number of girls also came to help finish the cleaning process and package them for the freezer.

The machine did a wonderful job, and the chickens came out very clean. This sped up our whole operation. I also saw that some of the older boys had become quite responsible with the killing and scalding, freeing me to oversee more of the final cleaning and packaging. By late afternoon the last of the dressed broilers were placed into the freezer, and I sent most of the children to the orphanage to shower and change. I instructed them to get washed up for supper while I cleaned up and put the equipment away.

Pop! What was that noise? It sounded like a gun being fired. I gazed down toward the dairy barn where the sound seemed to have come from. I saw several of the older boys who had not been involved with the butchering, but I didn't worry because Steve Stoltzfus was standing among them. Just then I saw Steve aim his potato gun out over the back field and again there came that loud *pop!* The blur of a speeding projectile shot from the PVC barrel of his homemade gun and arched up over the barn and way out into the back pasture. The boys clapped each other on the back and laughed, delighted. I watched in fascination as they helped open the screw cap and sprayed in another load of hairspray.

"Hey, Steve!" I hollered from nearly a hundred yards away. "See if you can hit me!" I presented myself as a target by standing erect and spreading my arms wide. Remembering how fast that potato had flown, I was glad I was standing behind a heavy chain link fence. Even if he did come close to hitting me, which I highly doubted, at worst I would only be sprayed with a little potato juice. I'd just finished butchering one hundred broilers, so a little potato juice certainly wasn't going to matter.

"Naw," Steve shouted back, "I'd better not. It might hurt you."

"Aw, come on. You won't even come close," I called back.

Steve hesitated, then reluctantly took his plastic contraption powered by hairspray and its push-button igniter and steadied it across a fencepost as he pointed the barrel in my direction. The boys held their breath as they looked on. I stood there like Stonewall Jackson, my arms, head, and shoulders protruding above the protection of the fence. I began having second thoughts when, *pop!* At the sound of that gun I lost my nerve and quick as a flash dropped to my knees completely behind the protection of that fence. I peered through the chain link at the projectile flying my way. I could hear it hissing as it came. Although Steve had done a wonderful job of lining up on me, he hadn't properly anticipated the drop, and his "bullet" hit the ground ten yards short of its mark. Then I realized that Steve's potato gun hadn't been shooting potatoes at all, but the butt end of an ear of corn. *No problem,* I thought as the kernels knocked loose and flew in all directions. Then I saw to my amazement that the "bullet" had bounced off the ground and was continuing in my direction, still hissing. But I felt quite safe having the chain link fence between me and that advancing ear of corn.

One thing I hadn't noticed in my haste to join in the fun was that my chain link protection stopped eight inches short of the ground. That ear of corn whizzed perfectly through the gap and smacked me squarely on the calf of my leg. It stung something fierce, and I jumped to my feet. Much to the delight of the boys, I began dancing about, rubbing a very bruised leg. Steve, however, felt bad that he had listened to me in the first place.

On Monday, during the ten o'clock school break, David and several of his school chums gathered on the second-floor landing of the outside staircase. Looking out over the garden and farm, they began talking.

"I'm braver than any other boy in school," David boasted.

"You're always bragging," replied Iliuţă.

"You talk too big," said Iosif.

David climbed over the guardrail of the landing and looked at the ground twelve feet below. "See," he said confidently, "I have more courage than all the rest of you."

"You'd better be careful," spoke up little Marian. "You might fall and hurt yourself."

"Humph!" replied David, "Fall? Why, I even have the courage to jump."

"You'd better not jump! You might break your leg," cautioned Nicu, his brown eyes large with wonder and his voice serious with concern.

"So? If I break a leg at least I won't have to go to school," retorted David flippantly. He paused for a second, then grinned at the other boys—and jumped. The boys rushed to the guardrail and looked at the ground below. They saw David rolling about on the ground, clutching his leg in a vain attempt to alleviate the searing pain. Nicu ran to tell David's teacher while the rest of the boys dashed down the steps and gathered around their fallen comrade. Adults were summoned and quickly arrived on the scene. Gently they carried David into the nurse's station, followed by a large crowd of children, each trying to give his version of the story.

The foot was turned unnaturally to the side. David had indeed broken his leg. I curled a piece of heavy cardboard and fashioned a makeshift splint while the boys told Viorica the details of David's jump. Realizing that I would have to make a run to the hospital, I parked the gray Honda at the door nearest the nurse's station. At a suggestion from Nurse Viorica, I took two quarts of our homemade ice cream along as a tip to insure prompt medical care for David.

We were well received, as was our ice cream, and David was

soon on his way to the X-ray department. The films clearly showed a double break in the large bone of David's right leg, about halfway between his knee and ankle. The attending physician formed a more substantial plaster splint and ordered David to remain in the Suceava Hospital for several days until the swelling went down. Later his break would require surgery to insert a plate and screws.

The hospital wasted little sympathy on a bragging boy who had been so foolish as to break his leg to prove his courage to his classmates. David received all the medical attention he needed, but without the loving care and concern that would normally have been given a boy his age.

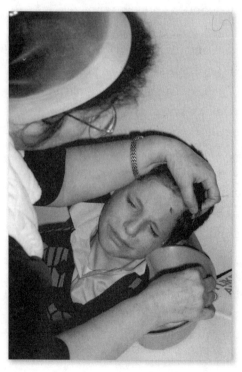

Nurse Viorica tends Costel's injury.

Peace reigned for one and a half hours following our return from the hospital, but was soon shattered by a horrible din from the nurse's station. Nine-year-old Costel had stumbled over a package being readied for the mail in our Gospel literature office and had struck his forehead on the sharp corner of Brother Willis's desk. It was a small cut, but bloody, and it drew instant attention from the other children. Costel appeared to be in more danger from lack of oxygen in the overcrowded examining room than from his head injury.

We were thankfully able to patch Costel's wound with butterfly bandages. Had it required stitches, we would have had to appear before the same hospital officials for the second time in one day. Besides gaining us a reputation for negligence, I feared we were beginning to run a bit short of ice cream.

After patching up Costel, I went back to my report. I needed to alert the CAM office in Ohio about the latest developments with David.

Waa! Waaaa!

Now what? I thought as I scrambled into the hallway once more. I met Tanti Tatiana, surrounded by no less than ten compassionate girls escorting their wounded comrade to the infirmary. At first I was hard put to determine which one was the victim, but Beti's cries were the loudest, and she held her finger as she cried pitifully. The nail was curled back out of place and the flesh was burst open. Nurse Viorica went to work immediately and patched her up using peroxide, iodine, gauze, and tape.

Beti had been exercising her usual powerful disposition in a "push-of-war" with the heavy steel doors upstairs. These doors separated the central room from the boys' and girls' dormitories. Beti had been determined to keep that door open, and Gigi had been just as determined to have it shut. Beti had accidentally curled her finger around the hinged edge of the door at the very moment Gigi had pushed.

Beti was not one to cry easily, so we knew the pain was excruciating. A dose of Tylenol took the edge off her pain, but nothing could alleviate the shame of having been bested by a boy in front of her peers.

We were thankful to hear from Cluj that Iulia's open-heart surgery had gone well and that they expected a full recovery, assuming no complications set in. Many prayers had been offered for Iulia as the children knelt at their bedsides, and God had heard those sincere prayers. Ionică reported that he would return as soon as possible, and that he was praising the Lord for the successful surgery.

Following Ionică's return from Cluj, his daughter called him from the hospital every day. At the end of their conversations she always said clearly, "Goodbye, Daddy." She had confided to her mother, "If I die, I won't have to go to heaven without having told my Daddy goodbye." Theirs was a special relationship indeed.

After three days in the hospital, David had surgery, and a plate secured the broken bone. Within a week he was back with us. We had no wheelchair, so we asked our maintenance man, Donnie, to cut a piece of plywood that would fit on the seat of the nurse's desk chair, with a portion protruding to support David's injured leg. Donnie did a fine job, and David was soon being wheeled around the orphanage by many willing hands. He loved the attention.

We had notified his father immediately after the accident. His father promised to visit as soon as he could. Soon David was able to walk again, but with a decided limp. The bones between David's knee and his foot were not quite aligned, and I feared that, without another surgery, he would limp for the rest of his life. Such is the price of pride in our lives.

As David's leg grew stronger, his old habits and wrong attitudes became more prominent. To our sorrow, we realized that although David had suffered much from his broken leg, his heart was still not broken before the Lord.

Finally his father came to visit. We talked with him about David's attitude, as well as his leg. He spent most of the afternoon with David. By evening his father said, "If you are willing to let me take my son home, I am ready to receive him. He now has a stepmother to help care for him."

Ionică held a lengthy conference with David's father and explained all the details. Yes, both David and his father understood that once David left our care he could visit us, but he could never again become a part of our Nathaniel family.

David proudly announced to the other boys that he was leaving. He was going to live with his father, and he was very happy. I, too, would have been happy had I felt that David's father could really be trusted and that he cared deeply for his son. However, my heart told me this was not the case, and I felt ill at ease as I watched him follow his father out the door and through the gate.

Two weeks passed. Then one day I walked into the dining room and saw Iosif talking on the phone. After a bit I heard him say, "You want speak with Tata Johnny, yes?" As he handed me the phone, he said, "It's David."

"Hello, David," I said. "How have you been?"

"Real good," came his reply. "I like living with my father real well. He has lots of land and seven horses, and I can ride any time I want."

"Are you going to school?" I questioned.

"Only when I feel like it," he replied.

"How often is that?" I asked.

"Well, when I want, I go, and when I don't want, I don't go. I really don't like school," he responded.

Sounds like the same old David, I thought. "Do you miss the orphanage?" I asked.

"No," he laughed. "Why should I? I'm having a good time here." He was polite to me, but I could sense his restlessness.

David called the orphanage each week and spoke with his classmates. He would tell one after another about the wonderful, carefree life he was living. These conversations had an unsettling effect on the boys. They sent the message that one can do wrong and still be blessed.

During one call after David had been gone for two months, he told his friends how much fun he was having, then he asked to talk to Tata Johnny.

"How are you, David?" I asked. "We miss you."

"Oh, I'm pretty good."

Then he came to the object of his call.

"Tata Johnny," he began, "did you know that I'm not living with my daddy anymore?"

"You're not?" I asked, surprised. "Why not?" I was afraid he had taken his wrong attitudes and actions home, where his less-than-loving father could not tolerate them.

"Well, actually," he explained, "my stepmother isn't living with my father anymore either. We don't have good conditions where we are. Tata Johnny, could I please come back to live in the orphanage again? I want to come there to live if you would please let me," he begged pathetically.

Tears stung my eyes, and my heart went out to him. Oh, how I wished I could grant him that request! But I knew if we gave in it would likely cause many more to think they could run away and return if things became too difficult.

"Oh, David," I said, "I'm so sorry you left the orphanage, and I'm sorry that you are not able to live with your father. But I think you well understand why you are not able come live at the orphanage again. Ionică explained all this to you and your father before you left."

"Yes, I remember," came David's subdued voice from the other end of the line, "but I just thought I would ask." He paused. There didn't seem to be much more to say. Then, softly and sadly, he said, "Goodbye, Tata Johnny."

I swallowed the lump that rose in my throat. "Goodbye, David." There was a click, and the line went dead. My heart cried out, "O God, watch over David! Help him to remember the good seed that has been sown in his life! May it someday bear fruit for you."

CHAPTER 16

THE DRAWING

"Tata Johnny, can I be the *paznic's* (watchman's) helper tonight?" asked Ionuţ. "I haven't been for a long, long time," he pleaded.

"Oh, no," said Gheorghe, "I was supposed to be the *paznic's* helper last week, but Pavel took my place because I had a fever and the nurse wouldn't let me. So this week I am going to be his helper."

"But that's not right!" countered Ionuţ. "You were the *paznic's* helper twice since I was!"

"That's a lie!" said Gheorghe forcefully. "It was only once, and that was your own fault, 'cause you got to go with Steve to buy fertilizer and didn't come back in time."

"Hold it, boys," I said. "That's enough arguing. I will choose someone to be the *paznic's* helper, and there will be no more arguing about it. Understand? If you're going to get bent out of shape over this, then I'll shut it down and not allow anyone to help our night watchman."

The boys had a long-standing tradition of asking for the privilege of staying up all night with our night watchman. They helped him in many little ways as he kept the wood-fired boilers stoked and removed buckets of ashes and carried them up from the basement to the waiting wheelbarrow at ground level. Clothing that was washed and dried by the night tanti needed to be sorted and taken to the boys' dorm to be ready when they awakened early in the morning. Then, of course, there had to be a snack at some point during the night. And finally the *paznic's* helper had the task of waking the boys assigned to feed the calves and help with the chores.

Ionică usually appointed the *paznic's* helper, choosing a boy he thought merited the privilege. Of course this could only be done on Friday night so the helper could sleep in on Saturday. The boys loved being the *paznic's* helper. He was a good conversationalist who loved to tell stories. However, the boys were becoming more and more aggressive in asserting their "rights" to help the watchman. There just had to be a better way. I finally hit upon a fail-safe plan.

Armed with two one-pint plastic containers, I called a meeting with the boys in their dorm. I had them sit lining the walls of the hallway.

"Boys," I asked, "how many of you like being the *paznic's* helper?"

All hands shot into the air.

"Okay, I want you to listen carefully. I know some of you have had more turns at this than others. What I'd like is to have a system that is fair for every one of you, and here is my plan.

"In this container," I held it aloft for all to see, "I have twenty-five slips of paper—one for each of you. Only one paper has the word '*da*' (yes) written on it, and the rest are blank. Tonight each of you will take one slip out of this container. If you choose a blank slip, that means you will not be the helper tonight, and you will place your blank slip into this empty container," and I held up the second one. "The boy who picks the slip of paper with *da* written on it will be the *paznic's* helper tonight. Next week we will do this again, but I will keep track, and those who have been the helper already will not get to choose a paper until everyone has had a turn."

Smiles and nods of agreement were exchanged. However, I had one more stipulation. "If you do not choose the slip of paper that says *da* tonight and you argue or cry about it, you will lose the privilege of choosing a slip next week. Do you understand?"

"*Da, da*, Tata Johnny, we understand—we won't argue or cry," they chorused together.

"Okay, all of you get to your bedrooms, and I will come around with the containers," I instructed.

I went from room to room, and all went smoothly. Each boy drew a slip from the first container. Then, when he saw that his paper was blank, he soberly placed it into the second container.

"Well, maybe next time. You are one week nearer your turn," I said encouragingly.

The drawing went smoothly until someone informed me that six-year-old Adi was crying because he had drawn a blank.

"I am not crying!" Adi insisted, quickly wiping his eyes. I chose not to see his tears. He was so little, and he wasn't arguing.

I entered yet another room and held out the container for two very excited boys. They had been waiting for me. Iosif and Iliuţă crowded close. You could see the tension in their faces. Gingerly, Iliuţă put forth his hand and gazed at the ceiling in deepest concentration. Reverently he picked a slip from those remaining. He opened the folded paper and let out a whoop.

"*Da*, Tata Johnny! It says *da!*" he shouted.

"Shhhh," I said placing my finger to my lips. "Not so loud. It is bedtime, and some children are already asleep," I cautioned.

"But I am the *paznic's* helper!" he said, throwing his arms around me and giving me a big squeeze.

Quickly he slipped out of his pajamas and donned more appropriate clothing. Suddenly he noticed that Iosif looked a bit dejected. Going over to where Iosif was standing, he placed his hands on Iosif's shoulders. "Don't be sad—I'm sure you will get it next week. Bye," he said, giving a quick smile as he rushed out the door and down the steps in search of the night watchman.

The following week there was extreme anticipation as I entered the boys' dorm with my now famous containers. I told them I would start as soon as every boy was in his room, and a mad scramble ensued as they hurried to their beds. I went from room to room, allowing the boys to choose. When I got to Manu's bedside he asked, "Did you hear who is going to be the *paznic's* helper tonight?"

"Why, no!" I said in surprise, wondering if someone had tampered with my containers.

"Well, Costel is sure that tonight it is going to be him," he confided. Manu chose a blank, and I moved on to Costel's room, where I found Costel in a high pitch of excitement. He stood out among his roommates dressed in work clothes, while they were already in their pajamas.

"Tata Johnny," he gushed, "tonight I am going to be the *paznic's* helper!"

"What makes you say you're going to be the one?" I asked, wondering what lay at the bottom of this.

"Oh," he said, "I just know!"

"He is so sure," snickered Andi, "that he won't even put his pajamas on."

"You'll see! You'll see!" cried Costel, the color rising in his face.

Andi picked a slip, but shook his head and placed the blank slip into the second container. Leon took a slip and did likewise. Marinel chose a slip, looked it over, snapped his fingers, and said, "Missed it!"

I held the container out to Costel, but he refused to choose.

"Come on," I prompted.

"But I'm scared to choose," said Costel.

"Hurry," I said, "there are others waiting." I shook the container, jostling the remaining slips of paper.

Suddenly Costel said, "Okay," and reached hurriedly into the container and chose a slip. He unfolded it, glanced at it, then turned it over. He stared straight ahead for a moment, then swallowed hard. His eyes looked moist, and his jaw muscles worked. Slowly his fingers relaxed, and the slip of paper fluttered to the floor.

"Remember, don't cry," I warned. "You want to have a chance to be the *paznic's* helper next week."

I bent and picked up the wayward slip of paper and placed it with the others in the second container, then moved on to the next bedroom. As I went, I overheard Leon saying, "He's going to cry, for sure."

In the very next room Marius softly exclaimed, "I got it!" as he opened his slip. Excitedly he changed out of his pajamas and into his work clothes for the night. "Man, I'm outta' here!" he said jubilantly as he hurried down the hall toward the stairs, stuffing in his shirttail as he went. Nearly every bedroom he passed had a well-wisher standing in the doorway.

As I had moved from room to room, I had also told the boys goodnight. Now, with the task of choosing the helper complete, I moved on to the girls' dorm to join Ruth in telling the girls goodnight. As we progressed from room to room, we came to Ionela's room. She wanted to know who had been chosen to be the *paznic's* helper.

"Marius," I answered.

"It's not fair!" she cried suddenly. "When are you going to let the girls have a turn? You never let the girls have fun like that!"

I tried to explain that it wouldn't be appropriate for a girl to work alone with the night watchman. Her nine-year-old innocence stood in the way of her understanding, and we ended up having quite a discussion. Finally we moved on to the other rooms. None of the girls seemed ready to go to sleep in spite of the lateness of the hour, and they all wanted to talk.

We were nearly done when the tanti on duty found us and said, "Tata Johnny, could you come help Costel. He has been crying ever since you left the boys' dorm. He's just crying and crying, and I can't make him stop. Could you please come?"

"We're almost done here. I'll be right over. Tell you what— have him come to the conference room between the two dorms. I'll see him there," I decided.

Five minutes later I entered the middle room, where I found Costel with his face buried in the crook of his arm. He was leaning against the wall sobbing loudly. I glanced at my watch. It had been more than an hour since I had left the boys' dorm, and here was Costel still crying! I was exasperated with him. *He really shouldn't get by with this! Should I spank him?* I wondered.

Another voice within me prompted me to take the softer approach.

"Costel, why are you crying?" I asked softly.

His answer was unintelligible.

"Here," I said as I gently removed his arm so I could see his face. His eyes were bloodshot and his face was red and puffy.

"I want you to stop crying so we can talk about this," I said soothingly as I wiped the sweat from his forehead. I wanted him to feel through my touch that I cared.

"But I can't stop!" he wailed pathetically.

"I know it's hard to accept disappointment when you have really had your hopes built up, but all of us face this sort of thing," I consoled him. "Please try to stop crying," I continued, "and we'll talk about this."

I sat on a nearby chair and drew him onto my lap. I realized he was making an extreme effort to calm down, even though his body contorted with spasms and his breath came in sporadic gasps. I was overwhelmed with an urge to wrap my arms about this quivering nine-year-old and just hold him. As we sat thus, my mind began to review Costel's history. His mother, we had been told, lived in a small shepherd's shack along with several others. She had cared for Costel as an infant, but when he was three he had found himself in his mother's way as she sought a relationship with yet another man, so he had run with the sheep during his third summer. Nothing was known of his father. Costel never even knew his own father's name. His mother thought how much easier her life would be without him underfoot, and when an opportunity came to obtain her first television set, she traded her son, Costel, for the coveted TV.

Another family had adopted him for a short time, but his adoptive parents separated, and he became a ward of the state. He was eventually placed in the Nathaniel Christian Orphanage. Early workers reported that Costel would hug them fiercely and hang on to them as though he feared they might run away as the sheep had done when he was younger. Was it any wonder that his emotions were fragile? How would I feel if I had experienced similar circumstances? Once again I realized that God in his goodness designed mankind to be brought forth in a home where father and mother loved God and loved their children. Oh, what untold childhood suffering is caused by parents who deviate from God's design!

Costel had become quiet with just an occasional gasp. I gently explained that he needed to learn that there are times when our desires are realized, but there are also times when we are extremely disappointed, and we must learn to accept these experiences in life.

"Come," I said, taking his hand and leading the way to his bedside. I boosted him quietly into his upper bunk so as not to disturb the other boys. Then I stood beside his bed gently rubbing his back and talking to him in low tones until he was almost asleep. Finally I asked, "Is it all right if I leave you now?"

"Yes," he yawned sleepily. "Please tell Mama Ruth goodnight for me, will you?" Oh, how this poor little boy longed to be wanted—to be loved—to belong!

It was 11:30 before I finally arrived at the little gray house and found Ruth dozing in her chair. Ida, Franklin, and Caroline were already fast asleep in their beds. *What kind of family life is this?* I had to wonder as I prepared for bed.

Two weeks passed, and I wondered how Costel would handle the upcoming drawing for a *paznic's* helper. True to my word, I had made him miss participating the week before since he had cried. He had handled it pretty well, although I could see it was hard on him.

I went from room to room, giving each eligible boy an opportunity to draw a slip. I entered Costel's room. Leon drew his slip, but it was blank. Andi drew his, and it was also blank. Costel approached in his pajamas. As he reached into the container, he said, "I'm sure I won't get it this time, but I won't cry." He opened his slip and glanced at the paper. His eyes widened in surprise as he sucked in a deep breath, then he shouted at the top of his lungs, "I got it, Tata Johnny, I got it! Praise the Lord! Oh, hallelujah, I have it! Thank you, thank you, Jesus!" He was jumping up and down and twirling about. Then he grabbed me and gave me as big a bear hug as a nine-year-old boy can give. Next he ran to Leon and showed him the paper.

"Here," I said, "give me the paper and change into your regular clothes. I'm sure the watchman is waiting for you downstairs."

I finished my rounds on the boys' side and hurried to catch up with Ruth as she was telling the girls goodnight. I had only moved through two of the rooms when Elena appeared at the door and said, "Tata Johnny, my brother Marian says to tell you to come right away because Costel is crying."

"What for?" I asked in surprise.

"I don't know," she shrugged, "but he said you'd better come right away."

I started for the door.

"Wait," said Mariana from her bed. "You didn't tell me goodnight yet." She stretched her little hands in my direction. I couldn't resist. I went back to her bunk and whispered into her ear, "Goodnight Mariana. I love you. Sleep well!" I kissed her cheek. She held my cheek against hers for a moment, then released me to go take care of Costel.

When I arrived in his bedroom, he was taking off his regular clothes and crying. "Costel," I asked in alarm, "whatever is the matter?"

"The tanti said I was too loud, and she isn't going to let me be the *paznic's* helper tonight. She said I shouted!" he wailed. "And I didn't, Tata Johnny, I didn't!"

"Yes," chimed in Marinel. "It's not fair because he did get the *da* slip in the drawing."

"That tanti is always so bossy," said Leon.

"Now, boys," I chided, "let's not be talking that way. Come Costel. Put your *paznic* helper clothes back on and come with me."

"But the tanti said I'm not allowed, and if I don't obey her she'll give me a bad qualification for the whole week," he sniffled.

I realized that the tanti didn't know about Costel's struggles and didn't understand what Costel had been through two weeks prior to this. I would take a hand in this matter, then explain it to her later.

"Look, Costel," I said, "I am the orphanage director, and I am giving you permission to be the watchman's helper tonight. You were pretty loud, and maybe even woke up several children with your shouting, but I will talk to her. Why don't you get dressed and follow me."

Costel lost no time in getting dressed for the second time that night and willingly followed me until I gave him into the care of our night watchman.

I found the tanti in the kitchen and gingerly approached the subject of Costel being the *paznic's* helper. I acknowledged that he had been overly loud and explained that he was sorry, but he was just so excited that he had won the drawing that he couldn't help himself. I asked her if she was all right with me making an allowance for him under these circumstances, and she said she was.

That night before drifting off to sleep I thought over the *paznic* helper events and the fail-safe, carefree plan I had formulated. Then I thought about all the struggles and turmoil that had come with it, and I wondered if going back to just naming a boy to be the *paznic's* helper wouldn't be best after all.

CHAPTER 17

IDA'S PRAYER

Before we were asked to move to Romania, our daughter Ida Jane had been praying to find God's will for her life. She desired to become involved in some type of work that would allow her to minister to the lives of others. She saw our move as an answer to that prayer.

Ida had turned nineteen just two days before we boarded the plane to move to Romania. She was determined to master the Romanian language and put forth much effort in study. We realized she was making good progress when a friend who attended our church and had stayed at our house for the night made an announcement at our breakfast table the next morning.

"Ida, you must have been dreaming last night," she observed. "You sat bolt upright in bed and said, 'No, I cannot go because I'm too busy, and I just don't have the time,' and you said it in perfect Romanian."

Working in the kitchen and laundry gave ample opportunity for Ida to sharpen her newly acquired language skills by conversing daily with the cooks, educators, and children. She especially enjoyed devotional time with the staff. Being able to converse also helped her learn to know our workers well, and she became personal friends with them.

All of our full-time daycare workers were Romanians, partly due to legalities. But now there was a need for another worker, and I wondered if Ida could apply for the position. After checking with Ionică and the CAM home office, we were given the green light to give Ida the job.

Now, after several months of ministering daily to the needs of the children, Ida felt a great sense of fulfillment. She loved working with her children. It took a lot of creative thinking to keep a group of fifteen girls happily occupied for an eight-hour shift. They were inquisitive, and Ida's storytelling abilities served her well. She shared her experiences growing up in America. Golden opportunities were filled with Christian values as she taught them day after day. Talking and singing together proved to be delightful methods of teaching as they cleaned dorms, weeded the garden, and beautified the many flower beds surrounding the orphanage.

Late one afternoon Ida marched toward the garden with eighteen assorted children following her. They marched happily along in single file, each with their own bucket or plastic bag in hand, looking for all the world like a mother duck headed for the pond with her family of little ones waddling behind. One of the other workers hollered after her, "Ida, what are you doing?"

Ida shouted back with a grin on her face, "We're having a rock contest." Sure enough, as they arrived at a portion of freshly tilled garden, her "ducklings" were made to stand in a straight line. When she gave the signal, the race was on! Children bent over and began hurriedly picking up rocks. They scrambled about, competing for rocks to place into their bags. This was fun! Besides, there was a prize for the one who picked up the most rocks. Whether it was eight-year-old Daniel's long arms or his speed that won the day no one knows, but he was declared the winner, with over four hundred rocks collected. Some of the rocks were mere pebbles, but Ida counted them all, and Daniel received the coveted honors and the prized candy bar.

Picking peas or snapping beans often began with a proposal from Ida. "Let's see if we can have these done by lunchtime, then we will go for a hike." We were amazed to see how well the children learned to work under such supervision.

On a particularly warm afternoon in July, the beans had been picked. They had yielded well, but the snapping seemed endless. The children were hot, miserable, and tired. They had talked about many subjects and had sung many songs. The stories were running out and the singing had begun to lose its luster when Ida announced, "Let's see if we can finish these beans quickly. Then, if there's enough time before supper, I'll take you girls swimming so you can cool off."

"Oh, let's do!" chorused enthusiastic voices all about her.

"All right, I'll ask Ionică for permission just as soon as we've snapped the last bean," she promised.

This announcement caused a flurry of renewed activity as the children went back to work with a will. In record time the beans were finished. The boys cleaned up the bean trash while the girls washed the pots and pans and put them away.

Everyone was soon ready. Seventeen-year-old Mihaela Svaduneac and Tanti Rodica agreed to accompany Ida Jane to help manage the twenty girls who were going swimming. Caroline decided to go along too. Ida had in mind to give them pointers on swimming since she knew that only a few of the girls could dog-paddle, and none of them could actually swim.

Theirs was a happy lot as they trekked along the dusty road leading back to the Suceava Reservoir.

Laura asked, "Tanti Ida, will you teach me to swim better? I can't breathe when I swim, but I know you can. Will you teach me how?"

"Sure. In fact, I will give all of you girls lessons," Ida answered happily.

"I don't know how to swim either," announced Tanti Rodica, "but I'll sit on the shore and watch the children." Ida's eyes widened as she came to the sober realization that she was the only one among them who could actually swim.

The lake side of the dam was covered with concrete slabs which measured four square yards each and extended well out into the lake to prevent erosion to the dam. Upon arriving at the dam, Ida cautioned the children about the dangers. One sad day four years earlier, our neighbor's three sons had drowned near this very spot.

Ida made the anxious girls wait while she waded into the water to determine just how far out it was safe for the girls to go. It was difficult to stand upright on the steep, moss-covered concrete slabs, so she pointed out a mark on the nearby pier as a limit for the smaller girls who couldn't swim at all. Then, venturing out to where it was waist deep, she pointed out another mark on the pier. She shouted above their excited chatter, "This is as far as you are allowed to go out if you can swim a little." All seemed to understand, and the splashing and laughter began. What fun they had!

A number of the girls had never really tried to swim before, and Ida was determined to do her best to teach them. She demonstrated, lying flat in the water, face down, taking long, powerful strokes with her arms while kicking her feet rhythmically. At the end of each stroke she turned her head and gulped a quick breath of air. A number of the girls tried to follow her example and came up sputtering and laughing.

"Tanti Ida," shouted Laura. "Come help me. I can't do it!"

"Show me how too!" begged Paula. Ida was having a great time. The water felt so refreshing after working in the sun most of the day. The girls chased each other and frolicked about as they splashed and had a wonderful time together. From time to time Ida had to remind them that they needed to move back closer to the shore. The girls were very respectful and obeyed immediately.

An enjoyable hour sped past, and soon it was time to head back for supper. Ida wanted to take one long swim alone out into deeper water before drying off. Free from her charges, she swam out into the lake. When she felt herself tiring, she turned back. To her surprise, she saw Mihaela Svaduneac, Laura, and Caroline dog-paddling to meet her. They were obviously out way past the mark she had set for them. In alarm, Ida swam to meet them, warning them to turn back.

Ida watched in horror as the three girls faltered and Caroline went completely under. Laura stretched her neck to the limit. Her toes touched the slippery surface of the concrete slab as she, too, slipped under. Gulping for air, her mouth and throat filled with water, and she panicked. She reached for Ida and wrapped her arms about her in a death grip. Ida, already tired out from her swim, struggled vainly to stay on the surface with Laura's added weight. Mihaela tried to stand, but it was too deep, and she couldn't keep her mouth and nose above the surface of the water. She felt herself slipping off the mossy slab and into deeper water.

Ida recalled her lifeguard training in America. *Keep a level head, and get away from the panicking person that is drowning, or you will not be able to help him.* Using her utmost strength, Ida freed herself from Laura's frantic clutches and fought her way to the surface. She took in a deep breath. A vivid thought flashed through her mind. *If they should die, I could never live with myself. I will save them or die with them!*

With all her strength she pushed Laura toward the shore. As

she did so, her own feet slipped on the sloped underwater slab, and she went under once again. Ida fought her way to the surface for another gulp of air. Her arms felt like lead.

Underwater, Caroline frantically grabbed Ida's arm, and Ida hauled her to the surface, even though that action plunged her own head underwater once more. Mihaela reached back toward Ida as she slid into deeper water. Her fingers felt something and instinctively closed upon the skirt of Ida's swimsuit. Ida prayed one short, desperate prayer. "Lord, help me!" God instantly answered her piteous cry. She felt her big toe slip into a crack between two of the underwater concrete slabs. Would it hold? She prayed that it would. Then with all her strength she flung her sister Caroline toward the shore. By this time, Laura had enveloped her again. Desperately, Ida disentangled herself from Laura's clasp and pushed her shoreward as well. Feeling the tug on her swimsuit, she blindly reached behind her and took hold of Mihaela's arm. Using the last ounce of her strength, Ida pulled her toward shallow water.

Tanti Rodica, stark fear written all over her face, had waded out as far as she dared to assist them. She helped Caroline stand. Laura was struggling, trying to find her footing on the slippery concrete. She fell, and her friend Cristina waded out, took Laura's hand, and led her to shore. Caroline and Laura were sobbing and choking up water as Ida and Mihaela struggled shoreward. Finally they reached out to grasp Tanti Rodica's hand as she helped pull their spent bodies out of the water. The four girls collapsed on the shore, utterly exhausted. They pulled deep draughts of air into their oxygen-starved lungs. How precious it was to breathe! How wonderful to be alive!

We were sobered by this event, which could so easily have resulted in four funerals. But we rejoiced that God had spared their lives. Ida felt the effects on her tortured muscles for several weeks, and the struggle to stay alive created a close bond between the four girls that lasted many years.

In Waslala, Nicaragua, a young missionary smiled to himself as he glanced at the envelope in his hand. It was addressed to him in that familiar handwriting and postmarked "Romania." His heart skipped a beat.

Following much prayer, and after seeking the blessing of both of their parents, Edwin Hershberger and Ida Jane had begun writing three months earlier. This was the latest correspondence. He wondered what this letter would say. He could hardly wait for a few private moments to be able to read it. Finally the last patient was discharged from the medical clinic where he worked, but it was later than usual, and supper was waiting, along with visitors from the States. His letter would have to wait.

Later that night, in the privacy of his own room, a smile upon his lips, he tore open Ida's letter. He read in the flickering candlelight. But his joy quickly faded, and he gripped the pages involuntarily as he read of the near drowning. He skimmed ahead to see if everyone was all right, and a chill went up his spine. After devouring the entire letter, he went back and reread it more thoroughly. Then he noticed the date on the letter and realized it had been written seven weeks earlier. So much for the mail service between Romania and Nicaragua! Still, reading about this experience had shaken him, and he thanked God for hearing Ida's prayer.

CHAPTER 18

THE CATCH

One Tuesday morning just before school Ida Jane dashed into the house all excited. "Dad," she panted, "there's a parakeet out on the fence, and the boys are trying to catch it!"

"Oh, really?" I said. I was busy and not overly interested, knowing that a loose parakeet would quickly fly away and they'd never stand a chance of actually catching it. But when she returned fifteen minutes later and said, "Dad, you just have to come," I thought perhaps I'd best go take a look.

It was a brilliantly colored blue and white parakeet, and I immediately saw why the children had been reluctant to stop chasing after it and go to their classes. My mind's eye immediately conjured images of it sitting in a cage in the orphanage living room with children gathered close, making cooing noises as they tried to introduce themselves and win its friendship. *I have to catch this bird for them!* I thought.

Daniel and Iliuţă stood nearby watching as I eased closer to the fence upon which the object of our combined attention was sitting. The boys were dangerously close to being tardy for their classes, but couldn't tear themselves from the saga unfolding before their eyes.

I was able to get within four feet of the bird when it burst into flight with a flash of color and a loud, scolding squawk. It flew several yards farther away and landed on the fence again. Slowly I worked my way closer to our bird, but once again it flew off, only to land near its original perch. After two more such trials and errors, I was almost ready to give up.

"Oh, Tata Johnny, please catch him!" Daniel pleaded. "He's so pretty! I want him! You'll let me have him when you catch him, won't you? I saw him first."

"No, you didn't!" chimed in Iliuţă. "I saw him at the same time you did."

"Boys," I chided, "I'm not at all sure I'll be able to catch him, but if I do, he will belong to all of us. Now you boys get to school; you're already late."

Daniel and Iliuţă dragged their reluctant feet across the lawn toward the school building, watching over their shoulders every step of the way. Finally they entered the school, though I doubted they would be able to concentrate on their lessons.

Knowing that the coming cold weather would be the undoing of our feathered friend, I decided to try again. I found that, with patience, I could get within about two feet, but that was it. Again and again I tried, but to no avail.

As the parakeet perched on the fence facing me, I noticed it was blinking its left eye more often than its right eye. I supposed it was because of the bright morning sun shining into his left eye. Taking this into consideration, I talked very sweetly to our friend, inviting him to become a part of the Nathaniel family and telling him he would never be lonely again if he would just consent to come live with us. While I was explaining this, I slowly moved my right hand, placing it between the bright sun and the parakeet's blinking left eye. I waited breathlessly with my left hand poised for action only eighteen inches away. Then the parakeet blinked his left eye. As fast as my reflexes could respond, my hand shot toward the unsuspecting bird. His blinking eye opened, and in a flash he was off the fence and in the air. He almost made it—but not quite. My hand closed over him in midair.

Our bird didn't appreciate being saved from the approaching winter. He struggled and bit furiously, squawking all the while. I liked his spunk!

I took him into our little gray house and showed him to Ruth. After slightly clipping the feathers of one wing to reduce his flying ability, I released him to fly about our living room. At recess the children crowded into our home to see the newest member of our family. Of course they all wanted to hold him, but when I explained how hard he pinched with his beak, they thought it better just to watch.

The next day I took several boys along shopping for a cage for our *papagal* (parrot), as the children called him. Daniel and Iliuţă helped me pick out a nice cage. Soon he was installed in the living room of the orphanage where, true to my earlier vision, the children all crowded about trying to win his friendship. On numerous occasions I locked the front door and allowed him to fly about the orphanage's spacious living room. Although Daniel didn't become Papagal's owner, he quite naturally took over the feeding and cage cleaning responsibilities. For this he was amply rewarded

Daniel and "his" papagal

by the close friendship he enjoyed with our beloved parakeet. Papagal loved to perch on Daniel's shoulder and ride about the living room, much to the envy of the other children.

As the weather turned cooler, we started preparing for the coming winter. Wood had to be stockpiled for the mammoth job of heating the orphanage and school. Flower beds had to be prepared and put to sleep for the winter, potatoes stored in our root cellar, and the last of the root crops harvested from the garden. Apples were plentiful in the Suceava area, and Ruth began to hunger for apple butter. She figured our Nathaniel family might just like apple butter once they had tasted it. With the help of our Romanian friends, we were able to find a Gypsy metal worker who was willing to make several large copper kettles for us. They turned out to be beautiful pieces of hand-beaten copper art. These he fashioned without solder, crafting hand-beaten, watertight seams. We could hardly wait to put them to use.

I met a beautiful sight one day after lunch as I was walking up to the orphanage gate. Stela's white coat gleamed in the bright sunshine, and she held her head high as though she realized the value of the precious cargo she was hauling. A wagonload of happy children shouted, "Tata Johnny!" and waved as they passed. Ionică held the reins and expertly guided Stela through the gate and onto the national highway beyond. She broke into a fast trot as he slapped the reins against her back. The children shouted their joy and waved their goodbyes. They made quite a sight all bundled up in their colorful jackets and caps against the sharp September breeze. They were on an apple-picking excursion to the neighboring village four miles to the north.

Cars slowed behind the wagon and were greeted by enthusiastic waves from the children. Drivers smiled and waved in return as they switched into the passing lane and disappeared northward.

When they arrived at the orchard, Ionică coached the children on how to pick the apples. The trees were loaded, and children were soon clambering among the boughs picking apples and tossing them to those standing below. Soon more than a dozen gunnysacks were filled, tied, and loaded onto the wagon. When Ionică was sure they had picked enough, he gave the order to climb on board. Boys quickly filled their pockets with apples to munch on the way. They hopped on at the last minute as Ionică took the reins, bound for home.

Several evenings later our bakery rang with excited talk as the children, Romanian staff, and American staff gathered to cut up the apples in preparation for applesauce and apple butter. Someone started singing, and at least sixty voices took up the refrain. We washed, peeled, and cut up apples as we sang. Loredana started a contest to see who was able to cut the longest unbroken apple peeling. Soon there were a number of contestants. Meanwhile, I operated a small cider press improvised from an old sausage stuffer and a large square of cheesecloth. It was slow going, but we eventually collected nearly ten gallons of freshly pressed cider, which we poured into two of our copper kettles. We started the fires and left the cider to simmer slowly throughout the night under the *paznic's* watchful eye.

By morning half the cider had boiled away, leaving an excellent base for making old-fashioned apple butter. Right after breakfast we added the apples, stoked up the fires, and began the stirring process. The weather didn't cooperate very well, and I had to erect a canopy to protect us from a cold northwest wind and a day-long drizzle.

The children had heard of apple butter but had never tasted it, much less participated in making it. It was all we could do to restrain them from rushing en masse to "assist" us at the copper kettles. Ruth and Ida Jane wrote up a list of teams. Every thirty minutes a new pair arrived to take over the stirring of the kettles. Each new team had to be taught how to grasp the handle. "No, you don't make it go up and down like a hoe in the garden," I instructed. "Yes, you have to move it about and not just back and forth in the same path. No, you don't stir it round and round. That causes the apple butter to slop out over the sides and the unstirred sauce in the middle will burn."

It was so sweet to watch as they took their seats on the bench. With an air of importance, their little hands grasped the long handle along with ours as we gave them several instructive strokes. After a minute or two, they would push our hands off the handle. They wanted to make apple butter all by themselves!

We smiled to ourselves as we watched Marius and Beti sitting side by side on the bench, each running their own stirring paddles. They looked for all the world like a miniature elderly couple. They carried on such a lively conversation that they had to be reminded to keep on stirring. The nine-year-old twins, Leon and Ramona, made up another team, but argued much of the time. Leon was of the opinion that the apple butter would get done sooner if he stirred it faster, while Ramona chided her brother for not stirring slowly or steadily enough.

Ruth added the sugar and cinnamon and became the official taster.

Late in the afternoon the drizzle stopped and a canning table was set up. The apple butter was declared finished, and the boys brought their little wagons loaded with clean jars and lids. Willing girls helped fill the jars, and the boys carted off the finished product to the bakery to cool.

After the last jar was filled, Ruth ordered the bread. Ida Jane had baked a batch of fine homemade bread, and her timing was perfect. It was still warm when it arrived down at the kettles. The children all clustered about, barely able to wait their turns as Ruth broke the bread and handed out small chunks. Armed with these, the children needed little prompting to swipe the bread over the inner surfaces of the still-warm kettles. When the bread had picked up enough warm apple butter, they stuffed it into their mouths. Eight loaves of bread later, the kettles were clean, and the children had fallen completely in love with apple butter.

It would have been good to end on this note, but the apple butter still had to be boiled in the canner. Not all the jars sealed, so on Monday morning Ruth pleaded with me to set up portable gas burners and canners in the bakery to reseal twelve two-quart jars. Although my schedule was hectic, I hurriedly complied with her wishes, setting the burners in place and connecting the flexible copper tubing to the gas line. Upon completing this task, I rushed back to the more pressing needs of directing the orphanage and school. Ruth had demanding responsibilities as well, and was teaching a Bible class for a group of ladies in the afternoon. Shortly before noon she asked if I would shut off the gas to the canners in about two hours. I replied that I was willing, though extremely pressed for time.

The day passed, and thankfully the pressure of responsibilities diminished. Still, it was nearly ten o'clock before I arrived at the little gray house. By eleven, our exhausted minds and bodies begged for rest, and we prepared to retire for the night.

Just then the intercom crackled to life. "Is Johnny there?" Martha's voice broke the silence.

"Speaking," I replied as I picked up the receiver.

"I think we have a problem up in the bakery," she said, and I caught a note of urgency in her voice. "I just stopped by several minutes ago, and the bakery is filled with steam."

"Steam?" I asked in disbelief.

"Yes," she replied, "and I could smell apple butter."

"Hang on a minute, Martha," I said.

Turning to my dear wife, I asked, "You turned off the burners to the apple butter in the bakery, didn't you?"

"Why, no," she replied sweetly. "You said you were going to take care of that. Didn't you?"

"Oh, Ruth, I completely forgot!"

Speaking into the phone once again, I said, "Martha, we were canning the apple butter and forgot to shut off the burners. I'm afraid we have a real mess on our hands. Thanks for calling. I'll run up there right away!"

I ran up to the bakery, shut the gas valve to the burners, and opened all the doors to get rid of the steam. As the kettles had boiled hour after hour, the water level had dropped lower and lower. This had caused the water to boil harder. Eventually the apple butter within the jars began to boil as well. The jar lids allowed some of the pressure to escape, but eventually it built up within the jars faster than it could escape. Finally one of those two-quart jars cracked right at the waterline. It became an apple butter propelled rocket as it streaked toward the ceiling, where it shattered, spraying boiling apple butter all over the ceiling, walls, and floor. With that jar out of the kettle, the water level immediately dropped lower, and soon another jar-rocket launched. When I arrived on the scene, no less that six of those hard-earned, two-quart jars of apple butter had blasted all over. Our beautiful, golden-brown apple butter dripped from our once-

Nicu amidst the exploded apple butter

white ceiling and oozed down our tiled walls. Ruth and I slipped in apple butter as we surveyed the damage. I was so discouraged I was tempted to close the doors, get a good night's sleep, and clean up the mess in the morning.

Just then Martha came to see what had happened. After surveying the damage, she cheerfully said, "Well, let's get busy. I'll help you."

We walked over to the orphanage to get mops, rags, and cleaning supplies. There we met the *paznic,* who wondered what we were doing at this hour. Ten-year-old Nicu, who was talking with the *paznic,* didn't quite understand what was going on, but as soon as he realized the bakery walls were covered with apple butter, he headed for the pantry, tucked a loaf of bread under his arm, and dashed out the door toward the bakery, intent on a midnight snack. I had to run after him and engage all my persuasive powers to convince him that this apple butter was not fit to eat, thanks to the shards of glass.

Nicu was a good sport and joined the cleanup crew. We labored until 2 a.m. and fell into our beds with the satisfaction of knowing that the bakery was clean, though the cinnamon had stained the ceiling.

Ten years later, there was still a spatter pattern that had stubbornly withstood many scrubbings and several layers of paint. Oh, how often our sins leave stains upon our lives that last for many years! But, unlike the apple butter, when we turn to God, He washes away the stain by the blood of Christ.

CHAPTER 19

ICA

Six-year-old Ica wondered what was to become of her now as she ran into the darkness of the one room her family called home. She tripped and nearly fell on an uneven bump in the dirt floor. She glanced toward her father's bed, afraid he might see her crying. He wasn't there, so she flung herself onto the other bed and let the tears flow. She couldn't hold them back any longer. Her mother was dead! Ica thought she would choke as she gasped desperately for air between great wracking sobs.

Eventually her sobs subsided, and she became vaguely conscious of the odor of body oils from the stiffened sheet which had long covered the matted straw upon which she lay. She could feel those little things crawling around in her hair again. How she itched!

For as long as she could remember, she had shared this bed with her three older sisters. She didn't mind, for their bodies were warm, and the house was always damp and cold. There was never enough wood for a fire except when they had something to cook. It did not seem strange to her that at times they were without food, even though Father always had a bottle to drink. It had been this way ever since she could remember.

Ica had dreaded the beatings most. She thought it strange that her mother had to endure more beatings after she became ill than before. But then, there were also more bottles. Ica placed her hands over her ears, as though it would block out the horrifying memory of that last fight. Huge sobs engulfed her once more, and she tried in vain to close her eyes tightly enough to squeeze out the sight. The curses, the blows, the screams, and the blood were forever etched into her impressionable young mind.

Mother had been taken to the hospital, but now their neighbor said she was dead. She didn't understand "dead." They were going to bring mother's body back home again, but she couldn't walk, and she couldn't talk. Ica wondered numbly if it hurt to be dead.

Nine months passed after that fateful day. Ica vaguely recalled her mother's funeral. Her father drank continually. His bouts of belligerent cursing and beatings were interspersed with periods of sullen silence. She felt filthy. She was constantly tormented by countless living things crawling about in her hair and all over her body. They bit her, and she couldn't keep from scratching even though she had several patches where the skin was raw and oozing. And oh, how her head hurt!

Ica wondered about the man and woman who stood in their doorway. They had visited them the previous week and asked her father many questions. They had talked with her fifteen-year-old brother and her three sisters. Some of their questions were about her, and that made her very uncomfortable. They had talked about a place where many children lived together in a big house. They had said it was very nice at that place, but she hadn't trusted them, and she would certainly never want to go live there.

Now they had returned. She remembered the tall man and the nurse from the other visit, but now they had a younger woman with them. The tall man sent her sister Alina to fetch her father.

Ica got up to go with her sister. She did not want to stay by herself with these strangers. But the nurse stopped her.

"Just stay with us," she said. "We won't hurt you, and we want to ask you some questions. Remember we were here last week? We want you to come stay with us. We have worked out the details. So today we have come to take you to your beautiful new home. You will go with us, won't you?" she asked.

Ica sat with her head lowered, her gazed fixed on the bare dirt floor. *They came to take me to my beautiful new home?* she thought. *Never!* She looked up to speak, but met the nurse's gaze, which was filled with compassion and kindness. Not wishing to hurt the nurse's feelings, Ica said, "Tomorrow I'll go."

The younger woman walked over to her. She bent over and took Ica's hand. "Hi, I'm Martha," she said in a pleasant voice. "I live at the Nathaniel Orphanage, where we have lots of children. We have a barn full of cows that give fresh milk for our children to drink every day. We also have a school where the children go to learn to read and write. We have come to talk with your family about you coming to live with us. Wouldn't you like that?" she asked.

A shudder ran up Ica's spine at the thought of leaving her family. *No!* she thought frantically, *I'll never go with them!* Just then her father and brother entered, followed by her sister Alina. Nervously, Ica clasped and unclasped her hands. Two of her sisters sat beside her on the bed and began encouraging her to go. "Look," said her sister Corina, "if they would take me, I'd gladly go just to get away from this horrible place. But they won't take me because they say I'm too old, and they only have room for one more girl."

"Oh, Ica," chimed in Dorica, "I think you are so lucky. You must go! Look at these people. They are really kind, and I'm sure they will never get drunk or abuse you—they are real Christians. I like Martha, don't you?"

Ica wiped at the tear that had just washed a clean path down her cheek. First she looked at the big man who was speaking with her father. There was something in the sound of his voice and the steadiness of his eyes that made her trust him. Then she looked at the nurse. Their eyes met, and she saw that this woman really cared about her. She looked down and wiped away more tears with the backs of her dirty hands. Then she looked up at the young woman called Martha. Martha smiled down at her and Ica's heart warmed.

The big man was speaking to her father, and Ica listened breathlessly.

"We will take care of her," he said, "and provide for all her needs. We will teach her about God, and educate her just as if she were our own child. We will teach her work skills. We have all the necessary papers along for you to sign if you are agreed, and we can take her with us today. The nurse will look after her medical needs, and Martha will work with her daily. What do you say Mr. Nicolae? Are you willing to sign these papers and allow us to give Ica a good home?"

Ica stared at her father. Then she heard him ask her brother Florin, "Do we allow her to go?"

Florin glanced affectionately at his little sister and said, "Of course we'll let her go." At fifteen, he had seen enough to know that his father would never be able to care properly for Ica. Her father dropped his head and was silent for a long moment. Finally, as though he wanted to get this over with quickly, he said, "Okay."

Florin placed his arm around his little sister. "I'll come visit you at the orphanage," he said, and kissed her goodbye.

Corina gave her a quick hug and said, "I wish I could go with you, Ica. Goodbye!" Dorica and Alina both blinked back tears as they bade her farewell.

Little Ica walked up to her father and the tall man. "Goodbye, Father," she said. "I am going."

His three-day stubble scratched her tender face as he bent and gave her a quick goodbye kiss. Nurse Viorica wrapped little Ica in a blanket and carried her out to the waiting car. Once inside the car, Ica became very sober. It was the first time she had ever been in a vehicle.

As they drove farther and farther from her village, she fought in vain to keep back her tears. Every bump along the rough road sent sharp pains shooting into the back of her head, but the deepest pain was in her heart, for she was leaving home. This was a turning point in her life—a day she would always remember.

After nearly an hour they arrived at the orphanage, where Ica was carried into Martha's apartment. Her blanket and all her clothing were placed into a plastic bag to be burned, and she was placed in a tub of warm water.

At first Ica did not want to get into the water, but when Martha placed her own hands in the bathwater and swished them around, Ica did likewise. Still, it took much coaxing from Viorica before Ica would finally allow herself to be placed in the tub. Viorica began to scrub Ica with warm, sudsy water. And how she did scrub! The water turned gray, and Viorica drained it, refilled it with fresh water, and resumed her scrubbing. She washed Ica's hair over and over again with special shampoo. It was a hopelessly matted mess of lice deposits, nits, and egg casings. Viorica finally gave up trying to save her hair and called for scissors. She cut all of Ica's thick hair off as short as possible, then went back to scrubbing. Again the water had to be changed.

"What's this?" asked Viorica in surprise. Martha looked on in amazement as Viorica gently probed a large swelling on the back of Ica's head.

"Ouch!" said Ica. "That hurts!" The swelling had been hidden by the matted hair, but now looked like half a tennis ball, and Ica winced whenever Viorica touched it.

"How long have you had this?" ask the nurse.

"I fell a long time ago, and that bump just came," she explained simply.

Viorica made a clucking sound with her tongue, shook her head, and said, "We'll have to see a doctor about this."

After several hours of treatment, Ica was finally dressed in a soft nightgown and given a place to sit at Martha's table. Her body craved the nourishing food that was set before her, and she ate with a good, strong appetite. Finally Viorica left for the evening. The sun went down, and Martha and Ica were left alone.

Ica began thinking of the rest of her family and became very homesick. Yes, she was washed and clean. Viorica's gentle hand had applied ointment to those itching, raw places on her skin. The crawling things were almost all gone, and she was wearing a beautiful, cozy, flannel nightgown. Her hunger was satisfied, but there was an ache in her heart—an ache for her squalid home.

Big tears welled up in Ica's eyes and spilled unbidden down her soft, clean cheeks.

Martha called, "Ica, look what I have. These books are filled with photos of my family. They live far away in America. Come, let me show you."

Ica brushed away her tears and climbed up on the couch beside Martha. There she turned page after fascinating page filled with interesting pictures of happy children playing on swings, in sandboxes, and with toys. Suddenly there came a sound at the door.

"What was that?" Ica asked in alarm.

Knock! Knock! There it was again. This time Ica could hear people. She glanced at Martha, but saw that she was not afraid.

Martha explained, "These are the children from the orphanage, and they can't wait until your quarantine is over to see you."

Martha invited Ica to come with her to the door. "Hi," said a friendly face through the window of the door. "My name is Ionela, and I'm nine. Welcome to our orphanage!" she said with a big smile on her face. She stepped back into the crowd and Roxana came forward, flanked on one side by Maria and on the other by Larisa. They smiled and waved as they pressed their faces against the glass. Ica giggled when she saw how funny they looked with their noses pressed flat against the window. Then the children began to sing, and what beautiful singing it was! Ica loved it. Martha pulled up a rocking chair and cuddled Ica into her lap while the large group of children outside sang, "Jesus loves the little children, all the children of the world. Red, brown, yellow, black, and white; they are precious in His sight. Jesus loves the little children of the world!"

When they started a second verse, Ica couldn't stop smiling. She heard her own name being sung. "Jesus loves little Ica, with all of the children in the world. He brought her to her nice new home; now she'll never be alone. Jesus loves the little children of the world!" Ica glanced up at Martha and flashed her a huge smile.

Martha kept rocking as the children continued singing. When the children finally left for their rooms, Martha glanced down at the sleeping form on her lap. *Fifty-four!* she thought, mentally adding Ica to our large family.

That night Ica awoke twelve times. Each time Martha said, "I'm right here; let's sleep some more," and Ica lay down and went back to sleep.

The following morning Martha and Tanti Geta prepared Ica to visit the doctor about her lump. In spite of all the efforts of the day before, they discovered more crawly things moving about in what little hair Ica had left. Tanti Geta brought a razor and completed the job Viorica had begun. Another vigorous scrubbing followed.

The doctor carefully examined the lump on Ica's shaved head and announced that he would have to lance it. He felt sure it was an abscess. Taking his scalpel, he made a deft incision through the scalp and drained the puss. "This infection could eat into the base of her skull and do permanent damage, or even threaten Ica's life," he explained. "We need to treat it carefully." The doctor bandaged the wound and told them to return the next morning.

With the pressure released, the pain subsided, and Ica fell asleep on the way home.

Things were so different in Ica's new world. At suppertime Martha explained, "Before we eat, we pray and thank Jesus for our food. So let's bow our heads, fold our hands, and close our eyes."

This they did, and Martha prayed. Glancing at Ica as soon as the prayer was over, Martha noticed a smile of contentment spreading across Ica's face. This smile was repeated at every prayer session.

Ica soon felt free to speak of her family. She told of her aunt, who stole food that kind neighbors had given to the children and sold it to buy alcohol. Ica never referred to her house as "home," rather "the house from which you took me."

At the end of one meal Martha served ice cream for dessert. Ica picked up the spoon, examined it, and began to laugh.

"Why, Ica, what's so funny?" inquired Martha.

"Just look at this spoon! It's so little! I've never seen a funny little spoon like this before!" she laughed. "In the house from which you took me, we only had four spoons, and they were much, much bigger."

Martha realized that Ica had never seen a teaspoon before. Ica had thought all spoons were the size of the four soup spoons her family had shared.

Martha noticed that Ica was captivated by her own image in the mirror. She often spent fifteen minutes at a time gazing at her own reflection. Martha soon realized this was the first Ica had actually viewed herself in a mirror. Ica kept asking about her hair, wondering when it would grow back. A thread from her bandage unraveled, and Ica's fingers found it. She was excited at first, thinking her hair was finally growing.

Like a lone duckling, Ica wanted to follow Martha wherever she went. Martha's basement apartment was cool, so Martha went to the furnace room. Intent on starting the fire, Martha paid little attention to Ica until she spoke.

"Tanti Martha," she asked, "why are you starting a fire now? I'm not hungry."

Poor Ica was used to having a fire only for cooking, not for heating. How she must have suffered during those long Romanian winters!

Martha and Ica were invited to have supper with Willis's family. Following the meal, Ica was contentedly seated on Martha's lap, listening to the flow of conversation. Suddenly, without any explanation, she climbed off Martha's lap and walked out the front door and into the cold darkness beyond. Martha's heart skipped a beat. *Surely she hasn't decided to leave and find her own way back to her home, has she?*

The anxiety in Martha's voice must have been noticeable when she located Ica outside and questioned her. "But I was only going to the potty!" responded Ica in surprise. Martha chuckled as she informed her that this house had an indoor toilet.

Several months passed, and Ica was fully integrated into the orphanage routine. Two other girls had offered to double up to make a bed available for her.

We thought it would be good for Ica to visit her family, so one day Martha took her to her father's house. But when they got out of the car, Ica did not want to go in. She clasped Martha's hand tightly. Just then a neighbor called out, inviting them to drop by for a visit. Martha asked Ica, "Don't you want to go to your house first?"

"No," replied Ica. "Let's visit the neighbors."

After an hour, Ica was ready to go back to the orphanage, and again clung to Martha as though her little heart was filled with fear. She resolutely refused to enter her old home.

Ica felt very much at home with us. One day while I was working in my office, she ran in and snuggled up to me. "Why, Ica, what's the matter?" I asked, startled by the fear in her eyes.

"My father has come," she told me, "and he says he is going to take me with him! Please, Tata Johnny, don't let him take me!" she pleaded as tears rushed into her eyes. "Please don't let him take me!"

Instinctively, my arm reached around her shoulders, and it touched my heart to feel how hard she was trembling. "Ica," I said, "listen to me. Your father is not going to take you from here. I won't let him."

"But he said he would!" she interjected.

"No, I won't let him take you. He does not have the legal right to take you," I explained. "Now listen. Why don't you run up to your room, and I will have a talk with your father."

Ica poked her nose gingerly out into the hallway like a quivering little rabbit. She glanced furtively to the right, then to the left, but was too afraid to leave my office.

I walked to the door and looked toward the living room, where I heard her father's raspy voice ranting about our orphanage. "Go," I said, giving her an encouraging shove. She ran toward the side door, but couldn't resist one more glance in the direction of the living room. She looked like a wild animal running for its life.

Slowly I made my way to the living room, where a number of orphanage children were gathered. They were silent as Mr. Nicolae sauntered about, telling them and the whole world about this terrible orphanage that wouldn't even allow his little girl to come see her loving father. I listened for a time, then engaged him in conversation.

"Mr. Nicolae," I asked, "how many times have you visited your daughter here? And how many times have we brought her to visit your home? I'm sure you understand that we record each visit in Ica's permanent records. Would you like me to get them for you?" I offered politely.

"But you won't let her stay in her own home for even one night!" he argued, stepping closer and shaking his finger accusingly in my face. The smell of alcohol assailed my senses, and I thought it time for a little shock treatment.

"Ica doesn't *want* to stay at her home overnight," I explained.

"What? Are you telling me that my Ica doesn't want to stay in her own home with her own family?" shouted Mr. Nicolae as he rocked back on his heels, arched his eyebrows, and stared at me as though he was having a problem focusing on my face. He continued angrily, "You have turned my very own daughter against me!"

The children were overhearing everything, and I felt it was time to bring this contest to a close. "You see," I said, since I now had his full attention, "your daughter is afraid of you."

Mr. Nicolae marched about the orphanage living room in indignation, flinging his arms and shouting incoherently.

"One of you girls go get Ica," I said. "Tell her Tata Johnny wants her to come."

Within several minutes Ica entered the orphanage living room. She made a wide detour, keeping well out of her father's reach as she came to stand by my side.

"Here is my lovely daughter," her father said in quavering tones.

"Now, Mr. Nicolae, your daughter is here, and you may ask her yourself if she would like to come to your house for a vacation and stay overnight."

Moving closer, Mr. Nicolae modulated his voice. He sounded like a dedicated father who might well give his life for his child. "Darling daughter, certainly you want to spend vacation time with your family. Wouldn't you like to come and stay with us for several days?" he asked wistfully.

In spite of his drunken condition, my heart went out to him.

"No, I don't want to spend time at the house from which they took me," she replied. "I want to stay here!"

"But why? Why do you feel that way?" he asked. "Certainly you are not afraid of your sweet old daddy, are you honey?"

I felt a soft little hand slip into mine and heard a timid voice by my side clearly say, "Yes!"

"You . . . you are really afraid of your own daddy?" he asked in disbelief.

Again the small voice beside me answered, "Yes!"

"Oh, I cannot believe this!" he said. "What have I ever done to make you afraid?"

I felt it best to intervene. I explained that she was afraid of him because he had been drinking. I told him that the next time he comes to visit Ica, we would appreciate it if he would be sober. He declared that he hadn't had anything to drink. I challenged him directly on that point, and he reluctantly admitted that he'd had a little.

After telling Ica goodbye, Mr. Nicolae was ready to leave. Mumbling to himself, he crossed the parking lot and headed toward the gate. Ica, standing beside me, breathed a deep sigh of relief. Then, smiling up into my face, she asked, "Now may I go back to my room?"

CHAPTER 20

SHAKEN

Saturday morning dawned bright and clear, and I joined the children up at the orphanage for their traditional pancake breakfast. There was lots of chatter around the tables as the children, filled with energy, anticipated the activities of the day. So much interesting talk was going on that it was a bit difficult to quiet them down for our devotions.

Nenea Daniel shared a lesson from the biblical account of Jesus telling the disciples to cast their nets on the opposite side of the boat after they had fished all night and caught nothing. Daniel explained to the children how they should also obey God. A scurry of activity followed our song and dismissal as the children assigned to clean the dining room began working.

Several girls asked permission to go shopping in the bazaar with Martha. Marius said he wanted Danuţ to help him clean the horse stables and put down fresh bedding. Ruth asked if there might be a responsible boy willing to clean out and organize the little red barn where all the garden tools were stored, and Leon took on that job. I had a report to write and send to CAM in Ohio.

On the way to my office I entered the kitchen where our young cook, Lăcri, scurried about. She had just finished serving breakfast to fifty-four children and six adults and was already preparing food for the noon meal, as well as thawing chicken for Sunday dinner.

Lăcri smiled. "Ya, Tata Johnny, you want coffee, I know. I'm sorry I didn't make it already, but I will do so immediately, and when is finished, I will bring it to you. Ya?" she offered in her most intriguing Moldovan accent.

Lăcri was a marvel. An orphan herself, she had lost her mother at only two years of age and her father when she was sixteen. She had worked for the Nathaniel Orphanage as a cook for several years before we came to Romania. Everyone loved and respected Lăcri. She was very serious about her relationship with the Lord, and this spilled over into her relationships with others. Full of energy and always happy, her attitude was contagious, and the children loved helping Tanti Lăcri in the kitchen. I was thankful to God for such a worker.

"Oh, that's all right, Lăcri, I don't need coffee," I said. "I just thought if there was some, I'd take a cup. Please don't bother. You're very busy." I might as well have saved my breath, as she was already rinsing out the coffee pot.

I had barely settled into my office and started on my report when three little girls entered.

"Tata Johnny," said Ionela, "Several of us girls want to ride the horse. May we?"

"I suppose you may, if you've finished your work. I don't want you getting into trouble with your tantis."

"Sometimes the boys won't let us ride. They don't like to share," she complained.

"Maybe I'll ask Franklin to supervise the horse riding and allow everyone to have a turn. Do you think that will work?" I asked.

"Sure. Come on, girls, let's go!" Ionela said excitedly.

"Now, just a minute," I warned. "You have your bedrooms and bathrooms to clean and the hallway to vacuum before you are allowed to go down to the barn. I want to hear the tanti give a good report about you on Monday night," I said teasingly.

"You will," Ionela said, flashing me a winsome smile and grabbing Daniela and Florentina's hands. The three of them dashed up the hall.

I had come to love being surrounded by this hum of activity. Interacting with these children and watching them develop their understanding of God as well as their natural abilities was a balm to my soul. To observe them blooming under God's smile of approval was more than enough reward for all the toil and stress they brought into our lives. *Life certainly is good!* I thought.

When we had first come to work in the Nathaniel Christian Orphanage, the children had all called me Nenea Johnny and my wife Sora Ruth. These were common titles of respect meaning *uncle* and *sister,* which they used to refer to other workers also. Little by little, however, I had noticed a subtle shift. Certain children began calling me Tata (Daddy) Johnny, and my wife Mama Ruth. No one suggested it; it just happened. I recognized this as a natural response to the close relationships that formed as their hearts became knit together with ours, much as they would have with the real moms and dads they had never known. In time, all the children and even the villagers began using these titles when addressing us. We gladly wore them as badges of mutual love conferred upon us by the children, and it warmed our hearts. Yes, life was certainly good!

But I had to get this report finished, so I tackled it once more. Thus absorbed in typing, I tuned out the activity as it swirled around me.

"No, no! You're not allowed to do that!" came a shout from the orphanage living room. It arrested my attention and I stopped writing.

"I can if I want!" came the indignant reply of a girl's voice. "He's not yours, even if you do think you own him!"

"But you daren't let him out! I'll tell Tata Johnny!" shouted a boy's voice.

I thought I'd best step in before the argument got completely out of hand. Upon investigation, I found that Florica had taken the parakeet out of his cage to let him fly about the living room. Daniel had discovered the empty cage when he had come to clean it and was quite upset.

"No one is to take Papagal out of his cage without permission from me," I said, explaining that if someone should happen to open the front door at the wrong moment, our parakeet would fly outside, and that would be the end of him.

"But, Tata Johnny, he likes to fly so much, and I just love to watch him!" interjected Florica, stamping her little foot in exasperation.

"I know you do, but we can't have children letting Papagal out of his cage whenever they feel like it. So always ask for permission first, okay?" I said.

Florica stomped off, crestfallen, leaving Papagal's recapture to Daniel and me. We chased him from one curtain rod to another until in desperation he flew down the hall and into my office, where he perched on top of my bookshelf, looking very pleased with himself.

"Great," I said to Daniel. "Let's leave him right there until you have his cage all cleaned and fresh water and seeds placed in their holders. Then you can come into my office and catch him."

"That's a good idea," Daniel agreed as he went back to his task.

A fresh cup of rich Romanian coffee awaited me on my desk, along with two chocolate chip cookies. Lăcri had more than fulfilled her promise. I munched the cookies and savored the coffee as I went back to work on my report. Fifteen minutes later I was interrupted as Melody Bontrager burst into my office.

"Dad is very sick! Can you come to our house?" she blurted out.

"Sure, I'll come right away," I promised.

"Bring a stethoscope. And hurry! Thanks," she said all in one breath. Then she was gone.

What could possibly be wrong with Brother Willis? I wondered as I snatched a stethoscope from the nurse's station and rushed through the living room on my way to the gray Honda. Oana and Larisa realized I was going somewhere and wanted to go along. They stepped right into my path as I dashed toward the front door.

"Tata Johnny, where are you going?" asked Larisa.

"May we go with you?" begged Oana.

"No, no! I'll tell you later," I said as I detoured around them and ran out the door.

Making sure no children were behind me, I hurriedly backed around and sped off. I pushed the gray Honda to the limit of safety as I drove the mile to Willis's house. I pondered as I went, *Appendicitis? Kidney stones? Gallbladder? What could it be?* I breathed a prayer for guidance as I bounced over the chuckholes. I cut the ignition, jerked the emergency brake, and was out of the car as it came to a stop. I dashed into Willis's house.

"He's in there," said his wife, Esther, clearly worried. She pointed to the first-floor bedroom. As I entered, I saw Willis lying on his bed, twisting and turning in deep pain.

"What's the problem?" I asked as I stood over him.

"Oh," he moaned between clenched teeth, "I feel terrible! There's so much pressure!"

"Where?" I asked.

"Right here," he gasped and laid his hand over his chest. "I've never felt this way before!"

"Tell me," I said, "how does your left arm feel?"

"It's kind of numb and tingling," came the dreaded reply.

He rolled and groaned as another spasm hit him. Several family members had assembled around his bed by this time. I glanced about the room and saw a large plastic bowl at his bedside.

"What's that for?" I asked, eyeing the receptacle suspiciously and recalling unbidden scenes from the emergency room where, years before, I had worked as an orderly.

"He was nauseated," Esther replied, "and the bowl was placed there in case he had to vomit."

When a heart attack was severe enough to cause immediate nausea, it was very serious indeed. It is the body's way of ridding itself of food needing to be digested, thus allowing more blood to be used to sustain life.

"Willis," I said, carefully choosing my words, "you are having a mild heart attack." I tried to soften the blow so as not to increase his shock.

A look of surprise crossed his face as he considered what I had just said. "No!" he said in disbelief.

"I'm afraid it is, and we need to get you to the hospital right away," I said.

We gathered around the bed and prayed. We committed brother Willis and his situation into the hands of our loving Lord. I asked Willis's son, Matthew, to get the Suburban ready with the back seats out of the way so we could lay Willis there. Romania had no 9-1-1 for emergencies. Besides, we could transport Willis to the hospital in less time than it would take for an ambulance to come get him.

Melody called Viorica to explain and asked her to meet us at the hospital. Moments were crucial. Matthew rushed in to tell us the mattress was in the Suburban and all was ready.

"Okay," I said, "we need three people on either side of the bed. We'll make a stretcher by rolling up the bedcovering and carry Willis to the Suburban."

"I can walk! You're not carrying me!" Willis immediately protested.

"No! You will not take one step out of this bed! We *will* carry you!" I emphatically informed him.

Willis's pain had diminished a bit, and we carried him out and nestled him into the back of the waiting Suburban. We took care to place his head toward the front so any sudden stop would tend to make blood flow toward his upper body. Steve Stoltzfus climbed into the driver's seat as Esther and other family members quickly filled the rest of the seats. I read tension and fear in everyone's eyes. All of us realized we were quite possibly in a race with death.

As we started off, I quietly instructed Steve to drive carefully and not take unnecessary chances but, at the same time, get us there quickly. Steve understood perfectly and did a fine job of maneuvering us around the worst of the potholes and through the traffic.

Suddenly Willis was seized with unbearable chest pain. I was so afraid he would die before we could get him to the hospital. Turning about in my seat, I placed my hands upon Willis and pleaded for God to spare his life.

The hand of God had directed Dr. Puşcaşu to take a house call that morning. He was a Christian doctor and had an excellent working relationship with CAM. He was highly respected by CAM and had received assistance and donated medicines from them. He was also a very busy man, and now he sat impatiently at a stop sign watching for a break in the stream of vehicles traveling the main thoroughfare. Suddenly he noticed a familiar Suburban speeding along as it wove its way in and out of traffic. It caught his attention, and he thought it highly unusual. At that moment he sensed a strong inner voice telling him to follow that Suburban. As soon as there was an opportunity, he did so, glad the large vehicle stood out among the smaller European cars.

Even then, he almost lost sight of it in the distance. Then his heart quickened as he realized it was headed toward the hospital. He followed as fast as he dared.

The guard at the hospital gate must have been informed of our coming, for he waved us straight through without the customary questions. Viorica was standing at the front entrance and motioned frantically for us to come there, bypassing the emergency room. We muscled Willis out of the Suburban on his makeshift stretcher, paying not the slightest heed to his protests or his declarations that he could walk. We carried him on his rolled-up blanket straight up the steps and through the main entrance of the Suceava Hospital, past all the curious eyes, and directly into the EKG room. In less than five minutes the machine was spitting out an EKG printout. A nurse held it in her hand and read it as it advanced from the machine. I saw her eyes widen as the printout told her what was happening inside Willis's body. Although I couldn't understand the orders she shouted in Romanian to her colleagues, I had no trouble understanding the tone of her voice and the urgency of her movements.

Dr. Puşcaşu suddenly appeared and took control. He immediately ordered Streptokinase—an artery-dilating, clot-bursting drug. He wrote the admission order and personally accompanied Willis to his room in the heart ward. The family trailed along soberly as the cot was rolled through the halls to the elevators.

We stood in hushed silence, impatient for the elevator to arrive.

"Willis is a very sick man," Dr. Puşcaşu told us. Then, looking at Willis's son Andy, he said, "Son, you won't be able accompany your father upstairs because of hospital policy, but you can tell him goodbye here. Slowly Andy approached his father. He kissed him as he told him goodbye. The elevator finally arrived, and I remained with Andy on the main floor while the rest of the family accompanied Willis up to the heart care unit, where he was wheeled into a ward with five other heart patients.

After being told we would not be allowed to see Willis, we returned to the orphanage to tell our large family what had happened and to ask them to pray.

Later that afternoon when we were talking things over on the phone with Dr. Puşcaşu, he said, "I thank the Lord that Brother Willis is responding so well to the medications. Do you realize that one year ago we had no such lifesaving drugs available here in Suceava?" He paused, then continued soberly, "When Andy came to tell his father goodbye while we were waiting for the elevator, I realized this could very possibly be a final farewell between father and son. It's that serious."

On Sunday, right after church, Ruth and I went with Esther to see Willis but were denied entrance to his ward. We waited patiently in the hallway, wondering why the delay. When we were finally given the go-ahead, we were informed that a thirty-four-year-old man had just been admitted following a heart attack very similar to Willis's. However, this man lived in a third-floor apartment and had walked down the steps to be brought to the hospital. A short time after being admitted to the bed right next to Willis's, the man had gone into cardiac arrest and died. They had closed off the ward to visitors until the paperwork could be completed and the body transferred to the morgue.

We were forced to realize just how fleeting life really is, and we thanked God all over again for seeing us though this crisis.

The orphanage children were constantly requesting prayer on behalf of their pastor, Brother Willis. Those prayers were not in vain. Willis experienced God's grace and recovered sufficient strength over the next several weeks to be able fly to Chicago with his family, where he underwent extensive tests and further treatment. After several months' rest, Willis was able to rejoin our staff and resume his literature distribution and pastoral duties in Romania. We praised God that he was able to experience a full recovery without open-heart surgery.

CHAPTER 21

SEEDS OF LOVE

The children were lined up in the hallway waiting as I entered the orphanage, obviously impatient to get to their seats around the dining room tables. I checked with the cook. Supper was ready. Snatching up the bell, I stepped back into the hall and paused for attention. There was a lull in the vigorous conversation, and I rang the bell, signaling permission for the children to enter. They filed to their respective places and stood for prayer. Conversations resumed in full swing as soon as the "amen" was said.

"Tata Johnny," said Roxana, her dark eyes shining with excitement, "did you know that Tanti Martha has a boyfriend?"

"Really?" I asked, feigning surprise. "And what makes you think that?"

"Because," chimed in Beti, "I saw Nathan Bange come pick up Martha Esh. I think he was going to take her to a restaurant, and he opened the car door for her."

"They're always talking together, and they'll probably be getting married soon," added Roxana.

"Now, girls," I cautioned, "you shouldn't be jumping to conclusions. I think you're just guessing about a lot of this. But let's suppose you are right. Is there anything wrong with two Christian young people getting to know each other better?"

"Oh, no, there's nothing wrong with it," snickered Beti. "It's just funny that they like each other."

"Well," I explained, "many years ago Mama Ruth and I were girlfriend and boyfriend too. We loved each other, and God has blessed us with a wonderful marriage."

"How old were you and Mama Ruth when you got married?" asked Roxana, her elbows on the table and her food momentarily forgotten.

"We were both twenty-one," I answered. "Martha and Nathan are older than we were. I think they are quite mature enough for this step in their lives, don't you?" I asked, smiling at her childish interest.

It was as though a family member was dating, and these little girls were excited with the romance of their "older sister." I was blessed with the thought that these children would be able to observe this blossoming relationship between our missionary workers. I knew Nathan and Martha had sought the Lord through prayer and counsel before pursuing this relationship. Years hence these little girls would hopefully put into practice the virtues gleaned through their keen observations.

Several weeks passed, and the children adjusted well to the idea of a special relationship between their Tanti Martha and Nathan Bange.

Some time later, Tina shyly entered my office and laid her glasses on my desk. "Tata Johnny," she began, "I lost a screw out of my glasses, and now the lens keeps falling out. The tanti tried to tape it, but Florentina bumped me at school and the lens fell out again. Could you fix it for me?"

"Leave them here," I responded, "and I'll see if I have a screw that will fit your glasses."

Tina left her glasses with me and skipped down the hall. I studied them more closely and found that not only was there a screw missing, but the threads were stripped. I was trying to figure out a way to remedy the situation when I heard my name.

"Johnny," said Ionică as he paused at my office door, "do you have time to come to the living room? There's someone here I want you to meet."

"Sure, I'll be right there," I responded as I carefully laid aside Tina's glasses and the tiny screw I was trying to insert into the frame.

I followed Ionică into the living room, where a well-dressed stranger stood. A small Gypsy boy stood nervously by his side, shifting his meager weight from one foot to the other as if he wished he were elsewhere. He was gaunt and hollow-eyed, as though he hadn't had enough to eat in a long, long time. His hair was cropped close, and scars were visible on his scalp.

Ionică motioned for me to join them and began explaining that Dumitru, a storeowner, had brought the boy to us hoping we might be able to provide a home for him.

Another boy? I thought. *But then, we can probably squeeze in one more. This one certainly appears to be in desperate need.*

The boy's large, sober eyes looked pleadingly up at me from under his heavy eyebrows. There was a forlorn look in his gaze, as though he was afraid for his future, but even more afraid of his haunting past. He watched and wondered. Could he trust these people?

Dumitru began the story. "Liviu lived with his mother and father, but they both drank a lot and often fought. At times they shouted curses at one another. That wasn't so bad, but when they resorted to screaming, pulling hair, and beating each other, he and his older brother, Vasile, would run and hide.

"The last time this happened, the fight turned even more violent, and his mother was taken to a special hospital for people with head injuries. Many months passed, but she never recuperated.

Liviu didn't know if she would ever be well again. His father was taken away by the police following that terrible fight and is now in prison. Liviu and Vasile went to live with their grandmother in the Gypsy village at Arbore, which is nothing more than a cluster of mud-brick houses on the bank of a shallow river. Liviu and Vasile were only there a few days before their grandmother announced that if they were going to stay with her they would have to pay for their own food.

"The very next morning she sent them off to beg in the large city of Rădăuţi, some ten miles away. At first Liviu enjoyed begging for money. Sometimes he told people his father and mother had died and that he was hungry. Other times he told them his father had been killed by a train and that his mother was very sick and needed the money for medicine. He could usually get more money than Vasile, perhaps because he didn't whine like the other street boys but always spoke politely to people, trying to win their hearts with his smile and his friendliness. Or maybe they just took pity on him because he was so small.

"At the end of one day he returned to his grandmother with a bulge of coins clinking in his pocket. His grandmother counted them, but then frowned and scolded him. She told him to quit playing around and start begging.

"Months passed, and Liviu received terrible beatings from his grandmother when there wasn't enough money for another bottle of whiskey. During his last beating, her walking stick raised burning welts as it struck his thin shoulders again and again and cracked against his skull. But the worst pain was caused by the words she hurled at him. 'Get out of here!' she screamed. 'Leave. I hope a train runs you over and kills you! I hope the wheels of the cars that follow will grind your body to bits and totally destroy you!'

"Liviu walked out of her hut, sloshed through the river, and made his way back to the city, promising himself that he would never go back to his grandmother's house again."

The child listened to this recital of his history with little emotion—just that pleading, wondering look in his eyes. Dumitru went on.

"By then, Liviu had been begging outside my store for a long time. I'd always looked out for the little fellow, making sure he had food to eat on days when begging didn't bring in enough. I noticed when he stopped going home and started sleeping wherever he was able to find shelter. I asked him about it, and he unburdened his troubled heart to me, explaining why he had stopped sleeping at his grandmother's house even though it was autumn and the nights were becoming uncomfortably cold. Many nights he slept on the bare concrete floor of an unheated apartment stairwell. Other times he had to make do with the hard bench at the train station until a policeman found him and chased him back out into the cold.

"Then, after nearly a year of begging, he no longer showed up at my store. I inquired among the street boys and was told that Liviu was too sick to come beg anymore. Alarmed, I searched for him. I was shocked when I found him, for he was very sick with pneumonia and had a raging fever. I took him into my own apartment. With the help of medicines I purchased for him and the tender care of my wife, we slowly nursed Liviu back to health.

"Now it is winter, and even though Liviu has gained strength, we just can't turn him back out onto the streets, but neither can we keep him forever in our tiny apartment."

Kneeling upon the floor so I could look directly into the lad's eyes, my heart was brim-full of compassion as I asked, "What is your name?"

"Liviu," came the lisped reply through his missing front teeth.

"How old are you?" I asked, needing to verify that he was within CAM's three- to seven-year age limit for admitting a child.

"Five," he shyly responded, glancing up at the man who had brought him.

"See," said Dumitru as he extended a roll of papers. "Here are the documents from the Department of Child Protection in the city of Rădăuți. I have heard good reports about the care given at the Nathaniel Christian Orphanage, and I hope you will be willing to take in my little friend. Liviu is a gentle, well-behaved boy, and would cause you no trouble. Please give him a chance."

I looked over the papers, and everything appeared to be in order. The birth certificate was missing, but Dumitru thought he could have it for us within a short time.

"We cannot take Liviu today," I explained. "We have to get permission from CAM's home office to take in another boy." I certainly felt this was a necessary case.

Ionică assured Dumitru that if permission was granted we would immediately notify him to begin the required blood tests and medical examinations. I asked Dumitru if he would be willing to keep Liviu in his apartment until we received word from the States, and he assured me that he would.

I shook hands with Dumitru and thanked him, then placed my arm around the little Gypsy boy who had already wiggled his way into my heart. I saw the glint of affection in Ionică's eyes as he told Liviu goodbye, and I realized that he, too, had been won over by this little street boy. We both desperately wanted to take this little waif off the streets and give him a good home.

I returned to my office and quickly repaired Tina's glasses. Then, taking advantage of CAM's Ohio office being seven hours behind our time, I typed up a report on Liviu and made a formal request asking for permission to receive him into our Nathaniel family. I was overjoyed at 8:30 that same evening when the fax machine squeaked into life and we received approval from CAM to bring little Liviu into the Nathaniel Orphanage. Praise the Lord! Liviu would be coming to live with us!

Ionică's face broke into a wide grin as I shared the good news. He immediately sent word to Dumitru, asking him to begin the medical tests and bring their results to the orphanage along with Liviu and his birth certificate. As soon as these were completed, Liviu would join us. The whole orphanage was buzzing with the news.

"Tata Johnny, what's he like?" asked Manu.

"How old is he?" Roxana wanted to know.

"Is he really a Gyspy?" asked Leon.

"Did his parents die?" asked Ovidiu.

"When's he coming?" asked Beti.

I tried to answer all their questions in turn, but at times they came too fast.

Nearly two weeks passed, and we heard nothing from Dumitru or Liviu. Then at noon one Saturday Liviu came with Dumitru and officially joined our great family. We were as happy to have him as he was to be with us.

That evening the children of the Nathaniel Christian School were to give their Christmas program for the orphanage staff and their families. We were caught in a frenzy of preparation. The final stitches were being sewn in the new dresses for the girls, and we were squeezing in one last practice for the nervous children and teachers. Liviu insisted on standing with the other children during the practice and trying to sing the Christmas carols along with them. He was hearing these songs for the first time in his life, but he still insisted on helping. He wanted so much to fit in and be a part of our orphanage family.

That evening, following a three-course Christmas staff supper, the school children lined up to begin the program. Standing at the end in the front row was our new boy. Little Liviu was dressed in black trousers that were a bit too large for him held up by a belt nearly a foot too long. His white shirt was of matching proportions. He held his head high and copied the other children's actions. As the children began to raise their angelic voices singing of the baby Jesus who so miraculously came to be our Saviour, it became evident that our newest child had only been with us eight hours. He turned and focused upon the singers standing nearest him. He was watching the shape of their lips for a clue to the next word in the song. While all the other children's lips were round with an O-sounding word, his little lips were still forming the P of the previous word. Throughout the entire song he was half a syllable behind.

I glanced about to see if others had noticed. As the children began their second song, the audience listened intently, but nearly every eye was on the little figure standing at the end of that first row. They saw how desperately he wanted to belong and how much he wanted to sing with the other children. They blinked away the tears that threatened to blur the touching scene before them and had to smile in spite of the lumps that formed in their throats. This same Jesus about whom they were singing had said, "Inasmuch as ye have done it unto one of the least of these my brethren, ye have done it unto me."

Liviu's serious, dark eyes momentarily swept over the audience as though he was trying to read their thoughts. *Why were they all staring at him? Were all these smiling faces really his friends? Or were they laughing at him?*

The program was truly a success—a wonderful way to introduce Liviu to his new family.

On Sunday Liviu attended church with us, and I was pleased when he wanted to sit with me. In spite of being a street boy, he took in the entire service as if he had grown up in a church.

That evening all the children gathered in the orphanage's

big living room, where we prepared to sing and have a time of fellowship. Alvin Stoltzfus and his family joined us. I looked over the crowd, but couldn't find Liviu anywhere. Turning to Ionuţ, who was seated to my right, I asked, "Where is Liviu?"

A feeling of alarm rose in my chest. I looked again just to make sure I hadn't missed him in the crowd. I had just opened my mouth to ask several of the older boys to go search for him when I felt a small hand patting my leg. Glancing down I saw little Liviu standing right beside me. He was asking if he could climb into my lap. With deep relief I gathered him into my arms, and we began to sing. The children sang enthusiastically, and Alvin told an interesting story to illustrate the Bible truth he was teaching. As I sat listening, I felt Liviu's little hand caressing my cheek. Then, on impulse, he reached up and, to my surprise, planted a kiss on my cheek. Liviu's short life had been so full of pain and turmoil, yet his heart was filled with love and affection toward those who showed him kindness.

We finally received Liviu's birth certificate and were rather surprised to learn that he was almost eight years old, rather than five as he had told us. Had he been warned that CAM would not take older children, or did he actually not know his age? Due to poor nutrition, children in Romania often do not lose their baby teeth until they are seven. I remembered Liviu's missing front teeth as I had knelt to talk with him at our initial meeting.

The following week Alvin discovered that, although Liviu was within a month of his eighth birthday and had never attended school, no one could accuse him of being a slow learner. Alvin was talking with several of his workers down at the farm while Liviu was standing nearby. Alvin used the number twenty in his explanation and had to smile as he observed Liviu glancing hurriedly at his right hand and nodding his head as he counted his fingers. Then he switched to his left hand and repeated the process. But the job was only half done. He kicked his right foot forward, remembering the digits in his shoe, and repeated the process on his other foot. Having successfully completed his calculations, he squared his little shoulders, and a look of satisfaction crossed his face.

Liviu sat next to me at the dining room table. I had to grin at the contorted facial expressions he made while lisping unintelligible Romanian a mile a minute. I never let on that I could not understand much of what he was saying, and he never indicated that he couldn't understand my mixture of English and poor Romanian. It was a well-kept secret between us.

Not everything about the new boy was sweet, and we soon saw the need to teach him more perfectly in several areas. One of those needs became evident when Franklin took the mare, Stella, out for a ride on a snowy day. Little Steluţa tagged along, and so did Liviu. Franklin tied the colt to the back of the wagon to train it and boosted Liviu onto the seat beside him. In a moment they were off. It was a beautiful day, and the sun made the snow sparkle as they took the country road back toward the lake. Liviu, as usual, was in a talkative mood and chattered nonstop.

As they returned and were nearing the orphanage gate, two neighbor boys suddenly began pelting the colt with snowballs. The colt jerked and reared in fright as the snowballs struck him in the side. Franklin was afraid this would make the already skittish colt fearful and hard to train. He jerked the reins and brought Stela to a sudden halt. Then he jumped from the wagon and chased after one of the boys. Upon catching him, Franklin gave him a good lecture that it was not only wrong but also dangerous to scare the colt, and he warned him not to do it again. The boy was sorry and apologized. Franklin released him and was returning to the wagon when his attention was arrested by an intriguing scene unfolding before him.

Liviu had taken it upon himself to defend his horse also. He had jumped from the wagon and run after the other boy. But when the culprit saw his small pursuer, he thought it wasn't worth the effort to run. So he turned to face the little fellow.

Franklin watched helplessly as Liviu jumped as high as he could, and at the very top of his leap swung his tiny fists, trying to hit the tall boy's face. Again and again he jumped and swung his little fists at the taller boy. "If I had a shovel from the barn," shouted Liviu with anger, "I'd hit you over the head with it, not once, but two times, to teach you a lesson!"

Franklin ran to the rescue and tried to calm Liviu down. He talked to the neighbor boy, explaining why it is not a good idea to throw snowballs at horses, and asked him to please refrain from doing so in the future. The neighbor boy sheepishly acknowledged his mistake and promised not to do it again. With that accomplished, Franklin turned and led the way back to the wagon.

Liviu immediately fell into step beside him and asked, "Did you hit the boy you caught? Did you beat him up real good?"

"No," replied Franklin thoughtfully.

"Why not?" asked Liviu. "He was smaller than you. You should have beaten him up real good." Franklin explained that he hadn't wanted to actually hurt the boys, only to warn them not to torment the horses again.

"Besides," Franklin continued, "the Bible tells us that we should treat all men with kindness, and even forgive those who treat us badly."

This was a totally new thought to Liviu. He had so many things to learn from his new friends. But one thing he knew for sure—he loved them.

CHAPTER 22

HEART BRIDGES

We had visitors at the orphanage again. This time it was of a group of thirty Romanians who had heard of our work with children and wanted to see it firsthand. I was a bit apprehensive to learn that their leader was a psychologist. I always had the impression that psychologists were constantly evaluating the people around them, and I never liked to feel that I was being analyzed.

"They're here, Tata Johnny, they're here!" announced Leon as he poked his head in at my office.

"Thanks, Leon," I responded as I rose to welcome our guests.

We began in the living room, where I introduced them to the marvelous way God had opened the doors for the Nathaniel Orphanage. I also explained how, through our assistance program for evangelists, we had learned of the needs of a number of children from more distant villages.

"Is it true," asked their leader, "that many children in orphanages are there because of alcohol abuse?"

"I cannot speak for the state orphanages, but alcohol figures strongly into about fifty percent of our children's home situations," I responded.

"How do you handle discipline?" asked the leader.

"We train, teach, and correct their behavior just like we would our very own children," I said.

"In 1991 when this land was purchased from the state farm, it was a trash heap," I continued. "It was filled with refuse from the village. People had been throwing their unwanted items and garbage here for years, and it was a very ugly place. Now as you look around the very same grounds, you see blooming flower beds, well-tended lawns, clean modern buildings, and many happy children. Numerous believers have worked diligently to bring about this transformation, and we are grateful to God for their dedication and help.

"Our children, too, in many instances, were unloved and unwanted," I continued. "They were thought of as worthless and considered trash—something to be disposed of. But God in heaven looked down upon these little children and sent caring people to rescue them. And just as the grounds here were transformed by the love of God moving in the hearts of dedicated men, so I believe God's love will take the ugliness of these children's pasts and transform it into a thing of rare beauty for His kingdom."

I could see mixed feelings gripping the hearts of our visitors as they pondered what they had just heard. Most were not believers, yet they were impressed with the thought of God rescuing unwanted children and making them into something beloved and precious.

With these thoughts throbbing in their hearts, we moved down to the farm, where they had many more questions. They visited the little barn where Stela and Steluţa lived with the Russian ram that had recently become a part of our extended farm family. They wanted to know how the children enjoyed the animals. I described how Marius loved to work with the horses and was responsible for feeding and caring for them.

"And the pigeons?" they asked, pointing to the screened-in

portion of the loft where four pairs of nesting pigeons were cooing in chorus.

"Those belong to nine-year-old Daniel," I responded. "He's the bird lover among us. Daniel has worked at little odd jobs, and with the money he earned he bought several pairs of pigeons from our neighbors. After they have hatched little ones, Daniel will let them out to fly about the farm. He knows that with little ones in their nests they will not abandon this barn."

"That will be nice. They are so beautiful!" observed a young lady from the group. "I just love to watch them fly."

"Hey! What's this?" asked our psychologist friend as he pointed into yet another cage.

We all gathered around a mesh-covered cage and peered inside. Staring back at us with huge, inquisitive, dark eyes were three young owls.

"Nicu caught these owlets. We will raise them until they can hunt for themselves, then we'll release them," I explained. "Now watch this." I bobbed my head up and down. There were peals of laughter from our visitors as the owls bobbed their heads in unison every time I bobbed mine.

"What makes them do that?" the psychologist wondered.

"I've never known what makes them respond like that," I had to admit.

The owlets

I led our visitors through the dorms so they could see the rooms where the children slept. They seemed impressed with the cleanliness and order. We wrapped up their tour in the dining room, where the psychologist asked me a very difficult question.

"Is it fair that you come here from America and these children learn to trust you? Little by little they come to love you, and you become an important figure in their lives. Then after a year or two you leave and tear their tender little hearts all over again—is that really fair to them?" he challenged.

I had never viewed this from a child's perspective, and with thirty pairs of eyes watching for my response, I hardly knew what to say or how to respond. I simply had no words. However, I opened my mouth, and the Lord filled it. What came out was unpremeditated and a surprise to me as well.

"I do not know how long I will be here in Romania. But as long as I am here I will do everything I can to build a bridge of communication and love from my heart to the heart of every child in this orphanage. Then, over that bridge of love, I will do my utmost to transmit all the godly values I possibly can so that, when the time comes that I must leave, these children will have something solid upon which to build their lives."

The dining room was silent for a moment as the psychologist, his group, and I contemplated this response. Then a look akin to awe crossed the psychologist's face, and he said only one syllable—"Oh."

He expressed in that utterance acceptance and approval of what we were trying to accomplish. He saw that our reason for coming to Romania was not to set up a showcase of childcare in which we could gloat, but to impact the lives of these children for God—because we cared. This labor of building heart to heart bridges and transmitting godly values had become the driving passion of our work with the children of the Nathaniel Christian Orphanage.

Livia had worked at the Nathaniel Orphanage for several years before we Millers came to Romania. We all loved and admired her for her dedication as a daycare worker. She was a rare jewel and a dedicated Christian. Her work with the children was much more than just a job to her. She had given her heart to these children, and they loved her in return. She demonstrated her love

Tanti Livia works with "her children" in earlier days.

for them in the way she played with them, sang with them, read stories, took them on walks, and prayed with them. Theirs was a special, close relationship.

Most of Livia's family had immigrated to the United States, but she was over eighteen, and the government had considered her an adult and denied her a visa. The love she would have showered upon her family members she poured out upon the Nathaniel Orphanage children instead.

But the years of separation had been painful, and Livia missed her family terribly. Now shocking news ran through the orphanage—Livia had been granted an immigrant visa! In just a few weeks she would leave us permanently to be reunited with her family in America.

Livia came to my office to tell me her final plans for leaving. She informed me emphatically that there was to be no farewell supper. Usually we held a farewell supper whenever a staff member left our Nathaniel family.

"I will finish my shift as usual and slip quietly away after the children are safely in their beds," she said. I could see the emotional struggle on her face.

"But why?" I asked. "Why would you even think of leaving without telling these children goodbye?"

Livia covered her face with her hands as she struggled to maintain her composure.

"I just can't stand to tell them goodbye," she said in a voice husky with emotion.

"But you can't just up and leave without giving them a chance to bid you farewell—you just can't!" I insisted.

Tears welled up in Livia's eyes, and she fled my office. I sat for several minutes considering what would be best. Suddenly thoughts of Jesus came to mind. He had taken his disciples out to the Mount of Olives. That farewell scene was clearly depicted in the book of Acts. Filled with that inspiration, I was spurred into action. I found Livia in the nurse's station wiping her tears.

"Look, Livia," I reasoned, "even Jesus, before he went back to heaven, gathered His disciples about Him and told them He was leaving. He instructed them one last time—remember?" I gently pleaded.

Livia turned to me, tears streaming down her cheeks. "Yes," she responded between fresh sobs, "but Jesus knew he was coming back!"

I saw through her tears that she was considering what I had said, so I left it at that.

The evening before her departure, Livia came to the orphanage

Livia's farewell supper with her "little disciples"

to have supper with the children one last time. She sat at the head of a table with her little disciples gathered about her. The discussion around her table was animated.

"Are you going to work for an orphanage in America?" asked Larisa.

"You're going to go live with your mommy, aren't you?" asked Florentina, her chubby chin sagely bobbing up and down and her sober brown eyes never leaving the face of her beloved tanti.

"Will you get married there?" asked Oana innocently.

"Tanti Livia, you will come back when we finish the first grade, won't you?" little Davucu asked, tears filling his eyes. He brushed them away on his shirtsleeve, but more immediately took their place.

Livia just enfolded him in her arms and crushed him to her. She felt an overwhelming rush of love for these children. The harsh realities of life had torn them from their own homes and loved ones. They had also keenly felt each loss when their two former directors had returned home to America. Each of those partings had left a trail of bruised and broken hearts. Livia hated the thought of her own departure adding yet another painful experience to their suffering. Life had been for them an endless series of painful partings.

"Do you remember, children," asked Livia, "when you prayed for me that I would be granted an immigrant visa so I could go live with my mother? Well, God has answered your prayers, and we shouldn't be crying about that, should we?" Davucu wiped his eyes on his sleeve once more.

Supper was soon finished, and the children clustered around Livia as she moved down the hallway and into the orphanage living room. Livia sat on the overstuffed corner couch with her children all nestled about her. Tina sat on her lap with red-rimmed eyes. The rest of the children gathered as closely as they could. Livia was crying softly, and the children were crying with her, even as they tried to console her. Davucu laid his head against her shoulder, and Maria stroked Livia's arm as she cried unashamedly. The children all felt the need to touch her. I felt a lump rising in my own throat. I had to swallow it before I could give the farewell blessing.

Later that night, following many gifts and words of appreciation, we parted tearfully, and Livia left. The children had been tucked soberly into their beds, and Ruth and I went from room to room to tell them goodnight. The atmosphere was understandably more subdued than usual. As we neared the far end of the girl's dorm, we heard deep, wracking sobs coming from the bunk where nine-year-old Maria slept. I tried to comfort her bruised, broken heart. Maria's mother had died when she was only a baby, and her father drank incessantly. There had been much pain and sadness in Maria's search to belong.

Ramona's head rose from her neighboring pillow as she propped herself up on her elbow. She explained, "Maria is so sad because her dearest friend Livia is going far away to America, and she will never see her again."

"This is really a blessing for Livia," I tried to explain. "We should think of how happy her mother will be to have her daughter living with her again." But Maria was crying so hard I wasn't even sure she heard me.

"Mama Ruth and I are here, and we love you very much," I continued, trying to console her, but none of my expressions of love and care seemed to have any effect upon her. She sobbed uncontrollably. I backed off and motioned for Ruth to take over.

Ruth wrapped her arms lovingly about the sobbing form and spoke tenderly into her ear. "Maria, I love you," she whispered again and again as she kissed her hot, wet cheek. "Try to stop crying and listen to what I have to tell you." But Maria cried all the more. "Maria, didn't you pray that God would give Livia a visa? Aren't you happy that she can go to be with her family?" But the wailing continued, and Ruth turned to me with her hands spread in a gesture of desperation.

At that moment we both turned at the sound of Elena's voice coming from the open doorway. "Mama Ruth, *roagă-te, roagă-te,*" she said as she pointed toward her sobbing friend.

"*Roagă-te?*" Ruth repeated to herself as she tried to recall that word from her language studies. Then it hit her. Elena was telling her to pray! Several months earlier, Maria had helped me understand Elena's request for prayer. Now the "bread" she had cast upon those waters had returned, and Elena, a ten-year-old slip of a girl with wisdom in the ways of God far beyond her years, was suggesting prayer to heal Maria's broken heart.

Ruth went to Maria once more and, holding her close, began to pray over her. She asked God to heal the hurt that Maria was feeling and to flood her soul with peace and comfort. As her prayer continued, the Master drew close and whispered, "Peace my child; be still." Within minutes, her little broken heart began to mend, and she soon joined the ranks of those who were already fast asleep.

That night as we walked toward the little gray house, I struggled to push aside the thoughts that forced their way into my consciousness. *It's only a matter of time before we will face what Livia faced tonight. How will we cope when it comes time for us to leave? How will we ever be able to do it, and what suffering will it cause these precious souls?*

I remembered the psychologist's question at the end of the tour, then I thought about the response God had placed on my lips. No, it would not be easy. Partings are always painful. But, remembering how Ruth's prayer had brought peace to a hurting soul, I knew in my heart that we were doing what God had called us to do. These partings were temporary. The bridges were forever.

As we neared our home, I cast my questions at the feet of Him who knows all, and left them there.

GLOSSARY

Adi	*AH dee*
Alina	*ah LEE nah*
Arbore	*AHR boh reh*
Bădiliţă	*buh dee LEE tsuh*
Beni	*BEH nee*
Biţica	*bee TSEE kah*
Bogdan	*bohg DAHN*
Bucureşti	*boo koo REHSHT*
Burdujeni	*boor doo JEHN*
Ceauşescu	*chah oo SHEH skoo*
Chibici	*KEE beech*
ciocan	*choh KAHN*
ciorapi	*choh RAHP*
Cip	*chip*
Cluj	*kloozh*
copii	*koh PEE*
Corina	*koh REE nah*
Costică	*koh STEE kuh*
Cotleţ	*koht LEHTS*
Cozac	*koh ZAHK*
Daniela	*dah nee EH lah*
Danuţ	*dah NOOTS*
Davucu	*dah VOO koo*
Dorel	*doh REHL*
Dorica	*doh REE kah*
Dumitru	*doo MEE troo*
Florica	*floh REE kah*
Gârdeşti	*gehr DEHSHT*

Geo	*JEH oh*
Geta	*JEH tah*
Gheorghe	*GE ohr gay*
Gigi	*JEE jee*
Hreaţca	*HRETS kah*
Iaşi	*yahsh*
Ica	*EE kah*
Ileana	*ee lee AH nah*
Iliuţă	*ee lee OO tsa*
Ioan	*ee WAHN*
Ioana	*ee WAH nah*
Ionela	*yoh NEH lah*
Ionică	*yoh NEE kuh*
Ionuţ	*yoh NOOTS*
Iosif	*YOH seef*
Iţcani	*ehts KAHN*
Iulia	*YOO lee uh*
Lăcri	*LUH kree*
Larisa	*lah REE sah*
Lavinia	*lah VEE nee ah*
Lenuţa	*Leh NOOTS ah*
Lipoveni	*lee poh VEHN*
Livia	*LEE vee ah*
Liviu	*LEE vee oo*
Loredana	*loh reh DAH nah*
Manu	*MAH noo*
Marian	*mah ree AHN*
Mariana	*mah ree AH nah*
Marinel	*mah ree NEHL*
Marius	*MAH ree oos*
Mihaela	*mee hi EH lah*
Mihai	*mee HI*
Mitoc	*mee TOHK*
Mona	*MOH nah*
Monica	*moh NEE kah*

Neli	*NEH lee*
nenea	*NEHN yah*
Nicolae	*nee koh LAH yeh*
Nicu	*NEE koo*
Oana	*WAH nah*
Ovidiu	*oh VEE dee oo*
papagal	*pah pah GAHL*
Parnica	*pahr NEE kah*
Pătrăuţi	*puh truh OOTS*
Pavel	*PAH vehl*
paznic	*PAHZ neek*
Puşcaşu	*poosh KAH shoo*
Rădăuţi	*ruh duh OOTS*
Răducanu	*ruh doo KAH noo*
Raluca	*rah LOO kah*
roagă-te	*RWAH guh teh*
Rodica	*roh DEE kah*
Slavă Domnului	SLAH vah DOHM noo loo ee
Ştefania	*shteh fah NEE ah*
Ştefi	*SHTEH fee*
Stela	*STEH lah*
Steluţa	*steh LOO tsah*
Suceava	*soo CHAH vah*
Sveduneac	*sveh doo NYAHK*
tanti	*TAHN tee*
Tărniceriu	*tuhr nee CHEHR yoo*
Tatiana	*tah tee AH nah*
Timişoara	*tee mee SHWAH rah*
Valentina	*vah lehn TEE nah*
Vali	*VAH lee*
Vasile	*vah SEE leh*
Vasilica	*vah see LEE kah*
Vaslui	*vahs LOO ee*
Vicov	*VEE kohv*
Viorel	*vee oh REHL*
Viorica	*vee oh REE kah*

ROMANIA

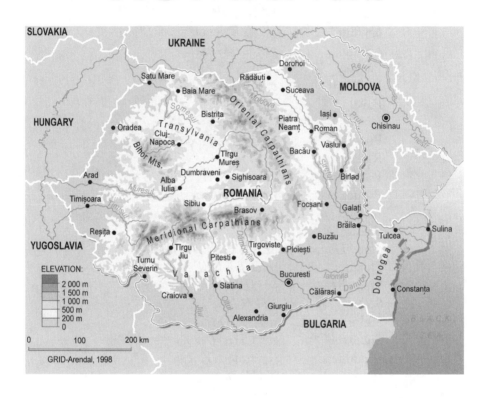

Map legend and labels:

SLOVAKIA
UKRAINE
MOLDOVA
HUNGARY
YUGOSLAVIA
BULGARIA

Dorohoi
Satu Mare
Rădăuti
Suceava
Baia Mare
Oriental Carpathians
Bistrita
Piatra Neamț
Iași
Chisinau
Oradea
Transylvania
Cluj-Napoca
Roman
Bihor Mts.
Tîrgu Mureș
Bacău
Vaslui
Arad
Dumbraveni
Sighisoara
Birlad
Alba Iulia
Mureșul
ROMANIA
Timisoara
Sibiu
Focșani
Galați
Brasov
Brăila
Reșița
Meridional Carpathians
Sulina
Buzău
Tulcea
Turnu Severin
Tîrgu Jiu
Tirgoviste
Ploiești
Pitesti
Dobrogea
Valachia
Bucuresti
Craiova
Slatina
Călărași
Constanța
Giurgiu
Alexandria
Danube
BLACK

ELEVATION:
2 000 m
1 500 m
1 000 m
500 m
200 m
0

0   100   200 km

GRID-Arendal, 1998

ABOUT THE
AUTHOR

In January 2007, Johnny and Ruth returned to Minerva, Ohio, where Johnny is a minister at Christian Fellowship Church. He works part time for his son, Dwight, who took over the family plumbing business when they moved to Romania in 1997. The rest of his working hours are spent writing for CAM. He hopes to finish his second book about the Nathaniel Christian Orphanage children by the time this one is published.

Johnny can be contacted by e-mail at johnny@emypeople.net or written in care of Christian Aid Ministries, P.O. Box 360, Berlin, Ohio, 44610.

ABOUT
CHRISTIAN AID MINISTRIES

Christian Aid Ministries (CAM) was founded in 1981 as a nonprofit, tax-exempt, 501(c)(3) organization. Our primary purpose is to provide a trustworthy, efficient channel for Amish, Mennonite, and other conservative Anabaptist groups and individuals to minister to physical and spiritual needs around the world.

Annually, CAM distributes fifteen to twenty million pounds of food, clothing, medicines, seeds, Bibles, *Favorite Stories from the Bible*, and other Christian literature. Most of the aid goes to needy children, orphans, and Christian families. The main purposes of giving material aid are to help and encourage God's people and to bring the Gospel to a lost and dying world.

CAM's international headquarters are in Berlin, Ohio. CAM has a 55,000 square feet distribution center in Ephrata, Pennsylvania, where food parcels are packed and other relief shipments are organized. Next to the distribution center is our meat canning facility. CAM is also associated with seven clothing centers—located in Indiana, Iowa, Illinois, Maryland, Pennsylvania, West Virginia, and Ontario, Canada—where clothing, footwear, comforters, and fabric are received, sorted, and prepared for shipment overseas.

CAM has staff, warehouses, and distribution networks in Romania, Moldova, Ukraine, Haiti, Nicaragua, and Liberia. Through our International Crisis program we also help victims of famine, war, and natural disasters throughout the world. In the USA, volunteers organized under our Disaster Response Services program help rebuild in lower income communities devastated by natural disasters such as floods, tornadoes, and hurricanes. We operate an orphanage and dairy farm in Romania, medical clinics in Haiti and Nicaragua, and hold Bible-teaching seminars in Eastern Europe and Nicaragua.

CAM's ultimate goal is to glorify God and enlarge His kingdom. ". . . whatsoever ye do, do all to the glory of God" (1 Corinthians 10:31).

CAM is controlled by a twelve-member board of directors and operated by a three-member executive committee. The organizational structure includes an audit review committee, executive council, ministerial committee, several support committees, and department managers.

Aside from management personnel and secretarial staff, volunteers do most of the work at CAM's warehouses. Each year, volunteers at our warehouses and on Disaster Response Services projects donate approximately 100,000 hours.

CAM issues an annual, audited financial statement to its entire mailing list (statements are also available upon request). Fund-raising and non-aid administrative expenses are kept as low as possible. Usually these expenses are about one percent of income, which includes cash and donated items in kind.

For more information or to sign up for CAM's monthly newsletter, please write or call:

Christian Aid Ministries
P.O. Box 360 • Berlin, OH 44610
Phone: 330-893-2428 Fax: 330-893-2305

ADDITIONAL BOOKS

BY CHRISTIAN AID MINISTRIES

God Knows My Size! *by Harvey Yoder*
Raised in communist Romania, Silvia Tarniceriu struggled to believe in God. But His direct answer to her earnest prayer convinced Silvia that God is real, and that He knows all about her. This book is excellent for family reading time.
251 pages $10.99

They Would Not Be Silent *by Harvey Yoder*
In this book, each of the stories about Christians under communism is unique, yet one mutual thread runs throughout—They Would Not Be Silent concerning their devotion to the Lord Jesus.
231 pages $10.99

They Would Not Be Moved *by Harvey Yoder*
A sequel to *They Would Not Be Silent*, this book contains more true stories about Christians who did not lose courage under the cruel hand of communism. It is our prayer that the moving stories will encourage you and help you to be stronger in your faith in the Lord Jesus Christ and more thankful for the freedoms we enjoy in our country.
208 pages $10.99

Elena—Strengthened Through Trials *by Harvey Yoder*
Born into a poor Christian family in communist Romania, after harsh treatment at a state boarding school and harassment from authorities for helping in secret Bible distribution, Elena finally decides to flee her home country. Will she make it? A true story.
240 pages $10.99

Where Little Ones Cry *by Harvey Yoder*
This is a story about war in Liberia. In the midst of the terror that war brings are the little children. Their stories, a few of which are captured in this book, are not of typical, carefree children. Some of these true accounts have happy endings, but sad trails lead them there. The purpose of this book is not to entertain, but to help you appreciate our blessed country more and create awareness of the pain and spiritual darkness that abound in much of Africa.
168 pages plus 16-page color photo section $10.99

Wang Ping's Sacrifice   *by Harvey Yoder*
The true stories in this book vividly portray the house church in China and the individuals at its heart. Read how the church—strong, flourishing, and faithful in spite of persecution—is made up of real people with real battles. Witness their heartaches and triumphs, and find your own faith strengthened and refreshed.
191 pages $10.99

A Small Price to Pay   *by Harvey Yoder*
Living in the Soviet Union under cruel, atheistic communism and growing up during World War II, young Mikhail Khorev saw much suffering and death. Often homeless and near starvation, he struggled to believe in God's love. This inspiring story of how Mikhail grew to be a man of God, willing to suffer prison for the God who loved him, will move you to tears and strengthen your faith. You, too, will come to realize that everything we can give to the Christ who saves us is still . . . A Small Price to Pay.
247 pages $11.99

Tears of the Rain   *by Ruth Ann Stelfox*
The moving story of a missionary family struggling to help some of the poorest people in the world—the men, women, and children of war-torn Liberia. Vividly descriptive and poignantly honest, this story will have you laughing on one page and crying on the next.
479 pages $13.99

Tsunami!—from a few that survived   *by Harvey Yoder*
Just like that, one of the greatest natural disasters in modern history approached the city of Banda Aceh, Indonesia. For most people, the cries of "Water!" reached them too late. But some survived to tell the story.
As you read the accounts in this book, you will experience, in a small degree, a few of the horrors that the people of Banda Aceh faced. Some tell their stories with sorrow and heartbreak, others with joy and hope.
168 pages $11.99

The Happening   *by Harvey Yoder*
The shootings at the Nickel Mines Amish schoolhouse shocked the nation and the world. This is the heartrending story of the young victims, their families, and the community as they struggled to come to grips with this tragedy. How could they find peace and forgive the man who had caused their grief? The true details of *The Happening* are woven into a story told through the eyes and heart of a young survivor.
173 pages $11.99

A Greater Call   *by Harvey Yoder*

Born into a poor family in famine-racked China, young Wei was left to die. But God had a different plan. Wei would one day answer a greater call. The cost would be enormous, but to Wei and other Chinese Christians, Jesus Christ was worth any sacrifice.

195 pages $11.99

Angels in the Night   *by Pablo Yoder*

Pablo's family had endured more than a dozen robberies during their first two years as missionaries in Nicaragua. But God had called them to Waslala, and they had faith that He would protect them.

In spite of the poverty and violence that surrounded them, a fledgling church was emerging, and a light, small at first but growing steadily, was piercing the darkness.

Angels in the Night continues the story begun in *Angels Over Waslala*, chronicling the trials and joys of this missionary family.

356 pages $12.99

In Search of Home   *by Harvey Yoder*

If Zumrat accepted the Christian God, her family would disown her, her husband would despise her, and she might even be killed. Still . . . what if this Christian God could give her the peace she longed for so much? The true story of a Muslim family's miraculous conversion, followed by persecution and a grueling journey in search of a place to call home.

240 pages $11.99

Steps to
SALVATION

The Bible says that we all have "sinned and come short of the glory of God" (Romans 3:23). We sin because of our sinful nature inherited by Adam's sin in the garden, and this sinful condition separates us from God.

God provided the way back to Himself by His only Son, Jesus Christ, who became the spotless Lamb that was "slain from the foundation of the world." "For God so loved the world, that he gave his only begotten Son, that whosoever believeth in him should not perish, but have everlasting life" (John 3:16).

To be reconciled to God and experience life rather than death, and heaven rather than hell (Deuteronomy 30:19), we must repent and believe in the Son of God, the Lord Jesus Christ (Romans 6:23; 6:16).

When we sincerely repent of our sins (Acts 2:38; 3:19; 17:30) and accept Jesus Christ as our Saviour, God saves us by His grace and we are "born again." "That if thou shalt confess with thy mouth the Lord Jesus, and shalt believe in thy heart that God hath raised him from the dead, thou shalt be saved" (Romans 10:9). "For by grace are ye saved through faith; and that not of yourselves: it is the gift of God" (Ephesians 2:8).

When we have become born again in Jesus Christ, we must be baptized and then be careful that we do not go back to our sins, since we are new creatures (2 Corinthians 5:17). "He that hath my commandments, and keepeth them, he it is that loveth me: and he that loveth me shall be loved of my Father, and I will love him, and will manifest myself to him" (John 14:21). It is important to fellowship with a faithful group of believers to strengthen and enhance one's Christian walk (1 John 1:7). Enjoy new life in Christ and be faithful and grow in Him (1 John 2:3; Romans 6:13; Revelation 2:10b).